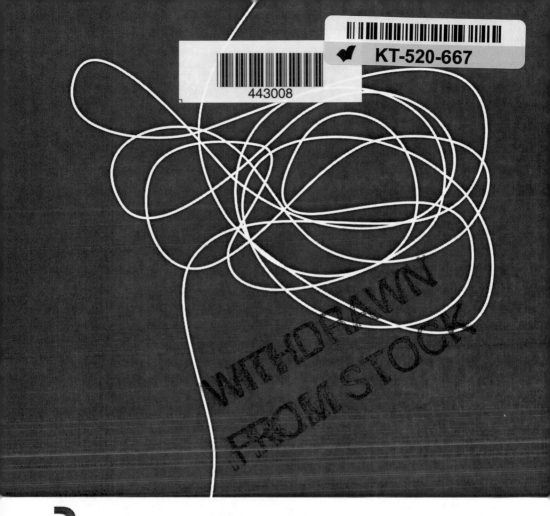

THE PRODUCER'S GUIDE TO
}TRANSMEDIA

How to Develop, Fund, Produce and Distribute
Compelling Stories Across Multiple Platforms

Nuno Bernardo

THE PRODUCER'S GUIDE TO TRANSMEDIA

How to Develop, Fund, Produce and Distribute
Compelling Stories Across Multiple Platforms

Avenida Duque D'Ávila, 23, 1º Dto.
1000-138 Lisboa,
Portugal
Phone: (+351) 21 3100142
Fax: (+351) 21 3100144

87 Waterloo Road,
Ballsbridge, Dublin 4,
Ireland
Phone: +353 1 4404205
Fax: +351 1 4430639

20 Hanover Square,
London, W1S 1JY,
UK
Phone: +44 208 0992962
Fax: +44 203 1782456

First published by beActive books in April 2011
Copyright © 2011 beActive books / Nuno Bernardo

ISBN: 978-0-9567500-0-6

beactivemedia.com

First Edition

THE PRODUCER'S GUIDE TO

}TRANSMEDIA

How to Develop, Fund, Produce and Distribute
Compelling Stories Across Multiple Platforms

Nuno Bernardo

To Triona, Martin and João.

About Nuno Bernardo

Nuno Bernardo is an award winning and Emmy nominated transmedia writer and producer and the creator of the world's first international interactive on-line teen series, Sofia's Diary.

After spending some years in the Marketing and Advertising world, Nuno Bernardo established his own Company, beActive, where he created "Sofia's Diary" (Portugal), a pioneering Interactive TV Series in its mix of traditional medias such as TV, Books and Live Events with new medias such as Internet and Mobile. The Series has been localized in 10 territories around the World so far and is distributed by Sony Pictures Television.

His pioneering work in this area has lead him to be guest and keynote speaker at International events such as the Toronto, Cannes and Venice International Film Festivals, MIPTV (Cannes), MEM (London), Participation TV (London), the Interactive TV Show Europe, Power to the Pixel, and many others.

In North America he is an executive producer for prime-time TV Series, including "The Line" featuring Linda Hamilton, and "Living in Your Car", which recently premiered on HBO Canada and will be broadcasted in the UK and other European countries.

Nuno's recent work includes Sofia's Diary UK for SONY and social Networking BEBO.COM and the second season of the Interactive show called "Flatmates" for the Portuguese Web portal SAPO and national broadcaster RTP that was nominated for the "Rose D'Or Awards". Flatmates is now being broadcasted in local versions in Greece and Romania.

In Brazil Nuno produced the Transmedia series "Final Punishment" which earned him an Emmy and a Rose D' Or nomination and a "TelaViva Best interactive Show" Award and a C21/Frapa Best Multi-platform Format Award. His work as the producer and creator of the series "Aisling Diary" for Irish broadcaster RTE also earned him two Kidscreen awards in New York for "Best Teen Drama".

Currently Nuno is producing the Transmedia series "Collider" and "Beat Girl" to be released by the end of 2011. In his home country, Nuno Bernardo already sold more than 500.000 books and his work is being licensed for International publishing. According to the BBC, "Nuno Bernardo is a leading world expert in New Media".

 www.facebook.com/transmediaguide

www.twitter.com/nmfbernardo

Contents

Foreword

by Liz Rosenthal (CEO and founder of "Power to the Pixel")

Technology is dramatically transforming the way that audiences experience stories.

For 100 years of cinema and 60 of TV, storytelling has been confined and restricted by distribution formats, running times and release windows. It is not storytellers who have created and defined the perfect shape or size to express their ideas but the industrial format or device where the story is experienced. Yet somehow we have convinced ourselves that the 90 minute feature film or the 52 minute made for TV episode is somehow the equivalent of the 'golden section' of filmic storytelling.

The Internet and the rise of an abundant array of free software, affordable devices and social media are tearing these preconceptions apart, transforming the way that we communicate with each other and how we tell, deliver and share stories. We're beginning to see the emergence of new forms of storytelling inconceivable before the Internet. This all offers exciting new opportunities for creators, producers and audiences.

This is the Gutenberg press multiplied ad infinitum. Monolithic media institutions are suddenly challenged with an audience who has taken control of its media. Audiences are no longer just passive viewers but are often actively engaged in the stories that they love, sometimes as collaborators in terms of co creation and fan fiction or avidly spreading the word as evangelical marketers and distributors. The fourth wall has finally been broken again.

The other huge change is that audiences are fragmented across multiple platforms, devices and activities. Younger audience are absorbing information in totally new ways, shifting effortlessly from one device or platform to the next and they want their media to be able to follow them. Wherever you sit in the life cycle of a story – creator, producer, financier, distributor or marketer, you need to be acutely aware of how to engage audiences in this increasingly fragmented world.

We are seeing three important forces coming together - stories, social networks and the gameification of nearly every element of our lives - transforming entertainment into something way more social than ever before.

Producers should no longer think in terms of creating stories for single formats but need to learn how to extend and build story properties that can engage with potential audiences across multiple media.

Yet cross-media, transmedia and multi-platform are clearly buzz terms in most media circles and often misunderstood as a fad or passing niche genre. And the powerful new tools of social media, mobile apps and real-time aspects of the web if adopted by traditional media companies are often left as a marketing after thought randomly strapped onto traditional linear formats instead of elements to be developed into the story to engage audiences from the beginning.

The possibilities that come from extending storylines, characters or scenes beyond one screen or a single format are exciting for the transmedia producer. There is an opportunity to increase the way in which a story can be discovered, reach new and wider audiences and build new partnerships and financing routes across the wider media, communications and tech industries

We are in a period of great flux where there are no established business models and consequently no rules however great opportunities for those with pioneering spirit. The sheer magnitude of new skills to learn can we pretty daunting for those who are used to operating in a traditional media environment. However what is the choice for today's producer as we see the devaluing of content in the connected and digital environment and the disruption and end of a cycle for the traditional TV and film businesses?

By developing new skills and having a close connection with your audience from the outset, as a producer you will empower yourself to extend the life and value of the properties that you create and build story properties that you can control more readily from the outset.

The Producer's Guide to Transmedia is the essential bible for those wanting to embark in this exciting universe. From a wealth of personal experience and rare achievement in this fledgling field, Nuno Bernardo candidly shares tips on producing, developing and distributing transmedia properties and succeeds in demystifying an often painfully jargon filled digital world.

Introduction
Growing Transmedia

When I sat down to write this book I had to ask myself two questions that I suppose every writer has to address at some point. The first question was why am I writing this? The second was who is going to read it?

Well, to answer the first question, I figured that I wanted to write something that would capture my experiences as I developed my own Transmedia projects. There are a variety of approaches to Transmedia, as you will see later when I set out some other valid approaches regarding the development of this type of entertainmen. My wish is to put on record my own approach and techniques and what I learned along the way as I developed products and grew my Transmedia business.

The second question concerns not just those who people interested in learning more about Transmedia but also, more precisely, those people who may benefit from reading this book. Generally, I hope that people working in the media sector will gain something from reading about my approach. More specifically, it is my intention that independent television and film producers, creative writers for different entertainment forms, brand managers and advertising professionals will see new opportunities - and, of course, new revenue streams - in the Transmedia storytelling approach that I describe here.

Getting started

I think there were two really important things that happened that lead me to start my own company and get involved in the Transmedia world.

The first was a presentation that I saw, in 2001, at the Millia Convention in Cannes. At the time, this particular convention was an annual event held to promote the best multimedia projects from around the world. Around this time, before the bursting of the Dot.com bubble, internet technology was the focus of a lot of attention from investors. At the same time, the internet, and its huge commercial potential, was still unexplored territory for most companies. It seems quite antiquated now, but the CD-Rom was the medium that was mostly used by multimedia companies. So, it was against this background of early development that I watched a presentation from Electronic Arts (a leading video games company) for a game called 'Majestic'.

Majestic was one of the first alternate reality games (ARGs), which were a type of game that blurred the line between in-game and out-of-game experiences. What made it amazing for me was the fact that they were using different media platforms for the same game. They were creating a really interesting story, but what made the game different was the way it sucked the player into the story by engaging them in a multitude of ways. 'Majestic' developed the concept that, even when you stopped playing, and had left the game and its world, the story would still go on.

This, for me, was a fascinating idea as it involved a completely different kind of thinking. Normally, you play a game for a set period of time and when you finish the game stops dead. Here was a game that had an entire world invented and constructed around it. This was a very developed, multi-layered world that you had to enter to play. What was even more remarkable for me at the time was the notion that this world didn't switch off when you switched the game off. In fact, the world was an ongoing thing and, because of this, the game would continue even after the player had stopped playing.

It was this idea, that the game's world was real and would go on regardless of whether you were present or not, that really intrigued me. The game achieved this sense of ongoing reality by texting players, calling their phone, leaving voice messages on their phone, even faxing them at their office. The idea was that, by engaging the player in such a way, the game would become a real, living entity.

This was completely groundbreaking and, for me at that time, breathtaking stuff. Unfortunately, for Electronic Arts, who spent a fortune developing it, Majestic was a complete commercial failure, largely because it was too ahead of its time. Another reason for its failure was because the plot was centred on conspiracy themes, which became slightly taboo a few months later in the post 9/11 world. As far as I was concerned, however, it was one of the most amazing developments that I had ever come across in the media and entertainment industry, and stayed with me long after I had left the convention centre in Cannes.

The second thing that launched me into Transmedia happened through a project I was working on after I had made that trip to Cannes. By this time, I was working on an interactive television pilot project in Portugal between TV Cabo and Microsoft. Microsoft at that stage was exploring the possibilities surrounding interactive television and were road-testing their products in Portugal before they took them to a global audience. Microsoft, at this point, was interested in how this would work technically but, as the project progressed, I became increasingly interested in how the different types of content were engaging and attracting audiences.

One of the things that I came to appreciate was, if you give the audiences something that is a bit more engaging than the regular television experience, they will really respond and connect with the content. I particularly remember one interactive card game that we were featuring that was more successful than the corresponding show on primetime. This multiplayer card game was quite simple in format, but allowed the player to interact with the game and other audience members in ways that were quite new at the time. It was also very novel for the time, in that it allowed the player to interact via a television set, as opposed to a computer or games console, while watching TV.

The interactive options it incorporated were fairly diverse for the time. For instance, there were options for an individual player to partner up with other players, play against others and chat to other players. Its success convinced me that, in a media world with an excess of stories, if you do something new, you can still capture an audience. Practically speaking, this for me meant that if you engage with them and give them something different they will watch your show.

Drawing lessons from that media convention in Cannes and my work with Microsoft TV, I realised that if you engage an audience and immerse them in your story you will gather a larger audience than you would otherwise. The reason for this is because it's far more enjoyable than the traditional passive narrative that they would be getting anywhere else.

First steps

Around this time, I decided to do something that would turn these rather nebulous concepts into reality. Accordingly, in late 2002, I decided to leave the interactive television project and start my own content production company called Beactive.

At Beactive, I started to develop this concept of engaging audiences with interactive content. Importantly at this stage I wanted this interactive content to be platform or media agnostic. By this I mean that I was focused on producing content but I wasn't concerned about what platform or media I would use to communicate it. My intention was at the outset that I would tell a story, preferably using several different media and platforms.

So, that was what was going on in the background, when I decided to develop stories that would engage with audiences in new and exciting ways. All I had to do, then, was figure out how I would do it.

As it happened, at the time a lot of people were beginning to focus on mobile phones as a new entertainment medium. This novel use of the mobile phone was growing exponentially, as audiences and consumers were beginning to use their phones for a growing number of different things apart from their primary communication function. It didn't take long to realise that the biggest consumers for this technology were teenage girls, who individually were spending a few euros per month on mobile phone content. I figured that one avenue to success could involve getting a story that would engage this phone-savvy generation of teenage girls.

Sofia is born

Arising out of this, one of the ideas we came up with seemed to tick all the boxes. It was decided to create a story following the life and adventures of an ordinary teenage girl through her diary. Now, the idea of following a character through a diary is a popular concept from the publishing world, but it also presented opportunities for what we wanted to achieve through new media. The diary also had the additional advantage of allowing us to publish content every single day.

Crucially, the way a diary story is told had, in itself, proved very attractive. A diary, which by its very nature is one event every day, slowly builds a narrative, until the sum of a few days tells a story. It was the perfect way to exploit the internet and connect with the audience, using blogs and new mobile services that would allow audiences to engage with a story in a revolutionary way. For instance, to engage with the audience, the character could perhaps text her audience about things that were happening during the day. Then, later that evening, the character could update her blog to reflect on the day's events and look forward to what was on the horizon the following day.

A text subscription service was to be available to Sofia's 'friends' who would receive these daytime updates, which would also act as a teaser for that evening's story. This was really important, as we knew an audience on the internet will not automatically come to you. You have to push the audience to go to your site and follow your story; therefore, the texts from the character to her audience were to be crucial if this was going to work.

In addition, we decided the daytime texts would allow the audience to interact with the story in the same manner as if the character was a real, living person. At this early stage, we were pretty happy with the basic media elements we would use and the form our story was to take. So, after finessing the framework of the story, we figured we would have to name this highly communicative character. Sofia, a teenage girl who shared her life with her friends through her diary, was born.

If at first you don't succeed…

Now that we had this fantastic idea, we set about developing it further and initially we tried the normal traditional route for getting the story to its audience. Accordingly, we tried going to a broadcaster and asking for money to develop Sofia's Diary with a view to broadcasting it. We went to a lot of meetings with broadcasters, told them it was going to be a huge phenomenon and that, in order for us to achieve this, we needed their money for its development and production.

I recall that everyone we spoke to in the various internet portals - broadcasters, mobile phone operators and so on - were very enthusiastic about Sofia's Diary. They loved the idea, saw the benefits of coming on board, and saw the great potential in the story and the production model. The problem was that, because it was an untried venture that only existed on paper, none of them wanted to actually spend their money and invest in it.

So, it was only after getting a sackful of rejection letters that we decided to produce the story in the only way that was open to us at the time. We decided we would launch Sofia on the internet, with some content being made available through a mobile phone subscription and also through a teen magazine aimed at our target audience.

…then try the internet

The internet was in retrospect the ideal place for Sofia's Diary to spend its formative existence. In a way, it was almost like a living production and development nursery for Sofia. On the internet we could create this brand, create the community and improve the concept.

Instead of just shaping the concept in a room with writers, we were shaping the concept every day with the help of the growing number of fans. This daily process helped us to shape and develop storylines and, as a team, get us into sync with what the audience liked and disliked about what we were doing. Even more importantly, it allowed us to tune into our audience to such an extent that we got to know what they expected from the story and characters. In this way, from day one we built on our audience feedback which, as it increased, became a vital improvement and development mechanism for the story.

Although we started on the web with a mobile subscription service and a magazine publishing extension, our goal was to create a longer-running series that would eventually move to other media. These plans included moves into television and radio and thus gradually transform the product into a well-known entertainment brand. Success on the initial launch media made this possible. The successful launch had proven both the attractiveness of our story and the viability of our approach. This success meant that, quite soon, we didn't have to go looking for other media to come on board with Sofia's Diary; instead, they were knocking on our door.

In fact, just under a year after we launched, we were getting calls from the same people who had previously rejected us. The television and radio broadcasters had heard about our success and now wanted to be part of it. You may be asking yourself how they heard about our success when our target audience was primarily teenage girls. Let me explain…

Getting noticed

If you publish a story on the web and acquire a dedicated fan base you will have achieved a measure of success. It's crucial, however, for you to realise that other potential media partners, including television broadcasters, probably will have no clue that you have achieved this. In fact, if you want anyone beyond your target audience to know about your product you are going to have to employ some good old-fashioned PR techniques. We encountered this issue early on and decided we had to plan a way for Sofia to break out of her niche and into the mainstream media.

Now, when I had started out with Sofia few people in the media knew about the character, the concept or the novel way in which we were producing the story. So, to raise awareness of Sofia, we decided we had to do something quite publicly that would get us noticed in a very elementary way.

Shortly after launching on the web, we set up a casting process to get a face for Sofia. We launched this campaign because, when we started, we still hadn't a face of Sofia, having initially launched with a silhouette illustration. In fact, part of the narrative at this stage was that Sofia was always saying she was very shy and periodically would ask her audience what they imagined she looked like. Then, she would ask them in particular what they thought she looked like. For example, did they think she had green eyes? Had she brown hair? Was she tall?

The next stage, after getting the feedback, was the launch of a nationwide casting process called 'Find the face of Sofia'. In this process, fans were asked to help us find the person who would then be the face of Sofia.

The process was incredibly successful, not only because we had thousands of fans turn up at the auditions, but also because the traditional media went crazy about the casting story itself. This was largely because we did the final casting in Lisbon, where a thousand kids eventually queued up outside our studios. Now, when you have this number of people turning up for any event you will block a bit of traffic, cause a stir and get noticed, and this is exactly what happened with the casting process. The PR buzz started and, having laboured largely un-noticed on the internet, we now found ourselves on the front of one national paper and being interviewed by national news channels. In short, people were sitting up and taking notice of us and Sofia.

Growing Sofia

Having broken through the traditional media wall, the decision-makers across the media industry now knew about us and soon the previously closed doors opened. For instance, in the weeks following on from the casting we agreed a book deal. The book deal was based on the blogs that had already been published together with some new content.

The book was published in August 2003 and turned into a huge bestseller, completely selling out on the first day and requiring three reprints during the first week. The publisher was, of course, very happy with this; from there we have gone on to publish sixteen books selling more than 500,000 copies in Portugal in this collection. The books were in every bookstore window, and the show was being mentioned in the mainstream media more and more.

The publicity at this point seemed to feed on itself. Though teenagers had known about Sofia's Diary for months, it was a completely new phenomenon on the mainstream media with the buzz surrounding this groundbreaking show generating a lot of curiosity. From this publicity, we also agreed a deal with two television stations (first a cable company in November 2003, then later the state broadcaster RTP in 2005).

During this time we also got a radio deal in January 2004. As if that was not enough, where we originally had a weekly column in a popular magazine for teenagers, we went on to publish our own magazine. We also released DVDs of the series and CDs of the soundtrack. Then, in 2006, we started doing our first licensing deals, where we licensed the production of things like pyjamas, mobile phone covers, t-shirts, fake tattoos – all, of course, with the Sofia's Diary logo.

The only media we hadn't used was the feature film. Though we got invited to produce a film, we never thought it would work because the market was quite small in Portugal. We also felt that the feature film platform wasn't really right for the Diary because it would have lost the intimacy that is necessary to sustain the narrative.

Sofia international

To be honest, when we started out we never envisaged the type of success we would achieve with Sofia's Diary. In fact, we had accomplished everything we could have hoped for after just two years.

As is typical for a lot of businesses, year one is about investment with some return on that investment in year two (if you're lucky). As things turned out, we achieved our objectives way sooner than we thought we would. For instance, we ended up producing Sofia's Diary in Portugal for five years, broadcast on prime-time television and even published our own magazine (which was something we hadn't envisaged at all).

I'm not saying all this as a boast, but more to point out that we hadn't fully envisaged this domestic success, and consequently had never really considered bringing Sofia to an international stage. This was largely because there was no precedent for formats being exported from Portugal.

In fact, across the industry at this stage, the future wasn't clear. The barriers to Transmedia seemed immense as each media has its own language, and audiences expect different content and experiences from different platforms. The barriers seemed all the more immense as few in the industry were talking about how these issues could be successfully dealt with.

As I say, going international was never part of our plan. However, at the same time I was getting increasingly exasperated at the media conferences that I used to attend, as they hadn't quite grasped the full potential of new media. Between 2001 and 2005 there was quite a lot of talk at these venues about the vast amount of content that could be available on new media platforms like the web, mobile phone, 3G and broadband.

I remember it was, for me, quite frustrating to attend these conferences and listen to media gurus talking about the potential of platforms and concepts for the industry without ever showing concrete examples of what they meant. Specifically, they never referred to the type of approach that we were using every day, where we were using multiple platforms simultaneously to tell a story.

So, I decided to do something about this. Before I went to one particular conference, I contacted the organiser and explained to them what I was doing and the type of production I was involved in. I told them that I doubted anyone else would be able to provide the type of concrete example that I could and that the conference delegates might like to hear about how we were producing Sofia's Diary.

Well, to say the organisers were unenthused with the idea is to put it mildly. However, after a bit of cajoling on my part, the organiser agreed to let me have ten minutes of speaking time at the end of one of the events, on the first day.

I only had ten minutes to explain what I was doing, but thankfully what I said generated some curiosity as a number of people told the organisers they wanted to hear some more about what I was doing. So, a few hurried arrangements later, I came back on the second day and spoke for about half an hour about what the Transmedia concept meant to me and how we were producing content across several platforms.

In retrospect, the buzz generated by that conference was another quantum leap for both Sofia's Diary and myself professionally. Without realising it, I had launched Sofia onto the world media stage.

After the conference, things took off internationally for us. The response was huge and kicked off a speaking tour of similar events around the world. The speaking tour also provided the opportunity thereafter to sell the format to media companies globally. We started signing deals and the Sofia's Diary format was then adapted to be used in different countries and territories worldwide.

As part of this process, we signed a deal with Sony Pictures and Television in the summer of 2006, and since then it has been broadcast in thirty countries in ten different languages. In 2008, we launched the show in the UK. Also, as we progressed we adopted the latest media technologies. For instance, the British launch allowed us to adapt Sofia's format to include new social media phenomena such as Bebo.

There was another significant consequence of going international with our format and explaining to people what I meant by Transmedia. It made me wonder how someone, such as an independent producer starting out, could use the Transmedia approach to gain an audience and create an extended franchise. It also forced me to look at what I meant by different terms and acknowledge that what we were doing was one path amongst many across the multi-media world that we live in.

This book

Before we launch into the detail of the book, I just want to say that it is intended to help a wide range of people and businesses from independent producers, television companies, film companies or broadcasters, to advertising agencies, brand managers, and marketers.

The book will, I hope, help others understand Transmedia in the first part. It will also help demonstrate how you can create your own Transmedia franchise from scratch or take your existing television or film product and make it more Transmedia. Alternatively, I hope it may also help you promote your brand using the Transmedia storytelling approach.

With these objectives in mind, I have grouped the content around four concepts to help you focus on what you want out of the book.

Part 1. Development (Chapters I-V)
The story development process is intended to help you figure out how to overcome the initial obstacles encountered along the way as you get your Transmedia project off the ground.

Part 2. Production (Chapter VI)
This aims to identify how you can grow your product and also how you can deal with the day-to-day production conundrums typical of the Transmedia process.

Part 3. Distribution (Chapters VII-X)
This part deals with how you can best bring your product to the market and the challenges thereafter as you expand. Finally, we will take a look at the pressing issues surrounding the changing landscape of the global media market.

Part 4. The Future (Chapter XI)
Changes in the media Industry that will affect the Transmedia producers.

Chapter I
Transmedia - A Perspective

-Why Transmedia?

-Some popular misconceptions

-Not the end of television

-Changing experiences

Transmedia - a perspective

Before you start developing your Transmedia product, it might be helpful to gain a perspective on what Transmedia means and how different people define it.

Broadly speaking, Transmedia storytelling involves creating content that engages the audience using various techniques to permeate their daily lives. In order to achieve this engagement, a Transmedia production will develop storytelling across multiple forms of media in order to have different entry points into the story. These entry points are the places where the audience can access content, with each point also providing their own unique perspective on the overall story.

This is a very broad definition of Transmedia. In reality, however, there are very many different techniques and approaches that all come under the Transmedia umbrella. To illustrate this, you may have noticed that, since the arrival of the new media age, industry commentators have been using buzzwords like 'multi-platform', 'cross-media' and 'digital media', and will often to talk about different aspects of what is generally described as new media. Therefore, if we are to discuss my approach to Transmedia we probably should try to distinguish it from other genres that are also spoken about.

Genre #1 - The Brand Extension

The term 'brand extension' encompasses some of the most successful entertainment models on television. Shows such as The X-Factor in the UK and American Idol in the US originated as successful television shows. What is important for us to remember is that the core of their existence is this television show and, although they have a website and mobile phones applications, these are all mere extensions of the core product. A brand extension will use these extensions purely to monetise and/or engage their audience for the short term. The extensions typically don't provide additional depth or an alternative perspective; they exist purely as gateways to the core product. In their most famous incarnations, they are successful, profitable and enduring. This a simple form of Transmedia, where a successful TV show, film or other big entertainment brand is extended to the digital world, exploring the IP in the new platforms. One of the jobs in the Transmedia World is to develop these 'brand extensions'.

Genre #2 - Made for the Web

In the latter part of the last decade, the webisode (video content for the web) and the mobisode (video content for mobile phones) became extremely popular in Europe and the United States. The webisode is a series with video content produced exclusively for the internet audience and released in serialised short-form.

Most of these projects are intended to form the prequel to a film or television series; alternatively, they are produced exclusively for the internet to be monetised in advertising. What happened with most of the projects, however, was that most of the projects were not adapted for film or did not make the jump into mainstream television. As for those produced exclusively for the internet, the online advertising was not enough to keep the projects going.

It remains a stand-alone industry with its own awards, known as the 'Webbys', but the challenges we have touched on remain true. It should be noted, however, that the aim of webisode producers to break into television is one that has borne results in a number of cases. On both sides of the Atlantic, commissioning editors have taken content made for the internet and commissioned television programmes based on that content. For example, the NBC's Quarterlife and Motherhood, which were aired on ABC.

Genre #3- The Transmedia Worlds

This genre is an evolution beyond that of the brand extension. It involves producers and creators going far further than the brand extension to create an entire world surrounding the original concept.

The process is frequently used by Hollywood studios to develop a movie and think about their story world as a whole and complete universe rather than simply focusing on just one story. In this process, the Transmedia elements act in accordance with the story universe, which contains a variety of other characters and storylines, rather than strictly following the original story elements.

This genre is exemplified by the big (Hollywood) franchises such as Pirates of the Caribbean, Star Wars and Avatar. These were hugely successful movies that opened up the possibility of creating revenues beyond just ticket sales into movie theatres. The movie studio takes the original successful movie story and then creates an entire universe based on that single product. The rules or bible for this universe determine what can be contained in it, what other stories exist in this universe. The universe is always being searched for these different elements and outputs, way beyond what was contained in the original story.

Finally, the studio decides how best they can monetise the wide variety of elements in this universe, i.e. how many characters we can write books on, what we can license to fast food chains as gifts, what video games can exist in this universe.

You can create endless sub-plots and develop characters in the bible that can then be licensed and monetised. The only rule is that they have to be consistent with what can exist in the universe as defined by the studio. In short, the Big Franchise is a stunningly successful example of how you can create an entire universe of applications after you have created a successful movie. Crucially, unless you are lucky enough to possess a Hollywood-sized budget, it is beyond most of us as a practical model. I will say, however, that this does present an opportunity for producers who want to work-for-hire producing Transmedia content in the film industry.

Genre #4- Organic Transmedia or the Original Transmedia Franchise

The approach which we will flesh out here involves a single narrative originally launched on a limited number of platforms, but which gradually expands across online and offline media to reach the maximum available audience.

In this case, the cross-platform activity grows organically from inside the story. As the product grows, the cross platform activities are not add-ons or gimmicks; instead, they are generated by the storyline itself. Likewise, the number of media distributing the story increases, but all the media will remain completely unified in terms of the overall narrative of the story.

When speaking about this genre, I will of course refer to my own experiences in creating projects such as Sofia's Diary, Flatmates or Final Punishment. These experiences and reflections on the challenges, successes and failures allow me to write this book and outline the approach.

A note on other matters

Before we go on to discuss Transmedia, I just want to refer to a type of content that is beyond our examination.

A vast amount of internet material is user-generated content. User-generated content, often humorous, is mostly unplanned and spontaneous and is very successful at gaining an audience. However, because it is unplanned and spontaneous it is extremely difficult to apply a business model to this type of content. Examples of these include the short film made for, or with, your mobile phone, user-generated content and also 'America's funniest videos' type content.

Again, the problem with these examples is that they don't possess any kind of viable business model. It is a product that engages the viewer for a very short period but, once consumed, provides no recurring revenue because you cannot contrive to recreate that type of genuine spontaneity. The material is often funny, generates internet traffic but is not commercially viable on its own.

Why Transmedia?

There are two compelling reasons for producing your product using a Transmedia approach. The first is financial, the second practical:

1. The financial imperative arises out of the increasing fragmentation of audiences across television channels around the world. The consequences for traditional broadcasters are huge because as they are faced with falling revenues and smaller budgets. The consequences for the independent media producers are also significant, as TV commissions inevitably become rarer and the traditional route of producing a television programme for a broadcaster becomes a less certain revenue stream. Basically, as I see it, if independent production companies are to survive they have to get the maximum financial return for their work. A key element in guaranteeing this return is the control and development of the product across multiple platforms, thereby generating alternative revenue streams.

2. The practical reason for going down the Transmedia route is that audiences are no longer confined to one medium. Audiences are already accessing content on alternative platforms and, as a producer, you have to go after them. This being the case, you need to engage your audience where they are. If they are no longer looking at the television then you have to seek them out on the internet or perhaps on their mobile phones. This presents a great challenge for traditional producers, who consider their only competition is the other television channels running at the same time as their show. With new media, you have to consider your competition among the bewildering array of distractions across an equally large number of media.

Some popular misconceptions

In the early days, many traditional producers said Sofia's Diary worked solely because it was aimed at a teenage audience that was tech-savvy. They said that it couldn't work with an older audience. At the time this was partially true, but only to a limited degree. For instance, I saw this with the interactive television card game (mentioned in the introduction) that we road-tested for Microsoft back in 2001. The interactive game was popular across the board, more popular than primetime television output at the time, and shouldn't be thought of as an isolated example.

Seven years ago, the internet had a huge penetration on younger audiences rather than older audiences. This, however, has changed significantly. Now, the penetration is huge across the board. Obviously it's still bigger in young audiences, but there is still huge (untapped) potential across older demographics.

As we developed Transmedia, we came to realise how great our entire audience was in the over-50s bracket. Feedback from fans showed that our story was a universal one that everyone could relate to. It was a significant lesson that we learned over time. We learned that if you have an engaging universal story you can break through any age demographic. Of course, the multimedia user penetration will still be higher with younger audience. However, it's worth bearing in mind that it is getting higher and higher with an older audience, especially as social media participation and wider internet usage increases across all age groups.

Not the end of television

All of this doesn't mean that the age of television is at an end. There are obvious examples of sports events, big national events and the big entertainment shows that will always capture large national audiences.

The key change, however, is that most other output can be supplied on demand. Drama, documentaries, and news are all essentially on-demand products. The trend is that this content will be increasingly consumed when the audience wants to consume it and not just when the television scheduler decides to broadcast it.

Audiences are by and large choosing the devices they want to use and the content they want to consume on them. Transmedia is valuable here because it allows you, the producer, to capture and engage with an audience. Crucially, it allows you to engage the audience in exactly the way that viewers are now accessing media content.

We, as media producers, have no option but to follow this accelerating trend. For instance, in the United States, audiences are now measured not just in terms of the television viewing figures for a specific programme; the audience figures are now also broken down into the various different ways the programme was consumed. For instance, they will measure not just the live broadcast figures but will also measure during the following week:

- Repeat transmissions and delayed viewings
- Personal video recorder viewings, e.g. Tivo in the United States
- Viewings on catch-up television services
- Viewings on the broadcaster's player services
- Viewings on on-demand services like iTunes.

In 2010, the figures showed a huge increase in television output being accessed online, on demand. The figures varied depending on the show; however, in the case of 'True

Blood', a hefty 40% of its audience accessed the show on non-traditional media such as on demand services, catch-up television or personal video recorder services. What is really remarkable is that a few years ago the figure was close to 0%. We have to ask ourselves, is it really so unlikely that the figure will rise further in the next few years? This not only creates advertising revenue challenges for the television industry, but also opportunities for television producers. We will talk about this later in the book.

Changing experiences

Later in this book I will talk in detail about how the way in which we define media is already changing and how this will affect us in the future. At this stage, I want to just note that, in the past, we defined our media experience by the device we consumed it on. This is changing, as viewers can now access different types of content, on any of their devices, meaning that the old definitions will no longer work.

That is why, when we are producing any type of content, we should concentrate on the experience rather than the device. The experience can be either passive or interactive depending on what the consumer wants at the time. I tend to classify these as being either belonging to the 'lean back experience' category or the 'lean forward experience' category. In the 'lean back experience', you lean back from the screen and consume it in a fairly passive manner. Alternatively, with the 'lean forward experience', content is consumed by a person sitting close to the screen, who is more engaged and at the time possibly multi-tasking.

Again, with these classifications the device doesn't define the experience; rather, the manner in which it is consumed does. The circumstances surrounding how you access the content have a huge role in how you access the content. The circumstances could be the time of the day, whether you are at home or in the office, are multi-tasking or solely consuming the content. You can take a range of devices such as the iPad, laptop or television and use them to access content in either a 'lean forward' or 'lean back' experience. For example, you can use both a laptop and an iPad in the 'lean forward' experience on your daily commute on the train. Alternatively, you can use these same devices in the 'lean back' experience to watch a television programme when you are at home relaxing.

Content producers need to note that this is fast-changing world where the device no longer defines the content. Accordingly, they need to produce content aimed at the specific needs of the consumer in mind rather than the device used to access it.

Chapter II
The Perfect Idea

- Where to start?
- Not every idea is a Transmedia idea
- What you can achieve with a small budget
- The never-ending story requires a big universe
- Three dimensional characters
- Small casts work better
- Contemporary is easier
- Remember how close you are to the viewer
- Be careful with Comedy
- Write it up

The Perfect Idea

Having set out some very broad concepts about Transmedia, I want to flesh out some guidelines that you may want to bear in mind as you start to develop your Transmedia franchise.

Where to start?

The initial key to making your story work is to make it stand out from the crowd. The key to this is to be original in the approach, if not the underlying concept. The mistake often made here, however, is the belief that an idea must be some sort of a gimmick to make it work. What I found is that, if a story brand is to have any kind of longevity, the original idea has to be underpinned by a story development plan that will sustain it over a long period.

The story development plan means that a lot of creative work is done to work out where exactly the story is to progress to. This is important because it can help avoid the pitfall common to many genuinely good, original ideas.

As an example, many new, original ideas have emerged in the past few years. I recall that when Sofia's Diary was in its infancy, around 2005, an internet phenomenon emerged that spread all over the world. It was the early days of the web-cam and soon there were dozens of teens talking in their rooms to cameras. There was a great excitement about this new distribution cycle. However, this success bred so many replicas that the phenomenon soon lost its novelty value. Thereafter, audiences for this type of content quickly fizzled out because everyone who first thought it was cute very quickly became bored with it. It was a new idea that simply ran out of steam because the original gimmick alone wasn't enough to sustain an audience.

The project ultimately has to have depth and be worked through and developed properly. The idea that 'I have a webcam so I can have a successful web series' simply doesn't work anymore. It has to be more than just the too familiar 'my friend the student filmmaker following me everywhere and documented my life'. Again, lots of these emerged but brought nothing new with them in terms of approach, so they quickly sank without trace.

I'm not saying that those other original ideas were bad ones. What differentiated Sofia's Diary from them, however, was that we had an original idea about how we would produce the story that was allied to a development plan showing how we would grow the characters and story over time. Our product wouldn't, therefore, rest just on one unique selling point, which was the new way we were producing a story. It would in fact be a story that would have, alongside its unique selling point, a plan to grow and develop both the characters and story over time. This development work, building up the story components, creates a much more complex product and is what sustains a Transmedia franchise.

Not every idea is a Transmedia idea

Around the year 2005 there was a misconception that all the ideas that didn't previously get accepted for film or television would work on the internet. This is not the case.

In fact, I still often go to Film festivals around the world where I'll invariably meet a few film scriptwriters who will tell me they have an amazing script for an online series. In many cases, I will find they have already been turned down by all the other media gatekeepers. Consequently, a lot of writers blame these media gatekeepers for the failure of the script to get commissioned.

The upshot of this is that, because the internet has no gatekeepers, many writers believe that it is the ideal place for their script to flourish. Sadly, this is not the case, as the internet audience has similarly high expectations that need to be satisfied if a show is to be a success. Consequently, I have found that, in a large majority of cases, these previously rejected scripts would also not form the basis for a good Transmedia series.

Similarly, I recall when a film-maker approached me about doing an online series about a young female rape victim coming to terms with her terrible experience. I told her it was a great television documentary, but it was simply too overwhelming for an online viewer who would have to engage with that level of trauma at close proximity. The point is, there are projects that make good movies and projects that make good documentaries, but not all of them will make for good Transmedia projects.

What you can achieve with a small budget

Remember also that even if you are a small company you can achieve a lot with limited resources. Creative management of your resources and writing will engage your audience. The Blair Witch Project, Paranormal Activity or the Irish film Once are all good, and quite different, examples of the type of success that may be achieved with a small budget using creative writing and clever production.

Understand that you are competing with the best Hollywood has to offer and then realise your audience won't tolerate unprofessional or sloppy writing. Whatever you do, don't try to make a cheap reproduction of your favourite big-budget series, because you simply won't be able to match the quality of the original unless you want to do it a parody.

The never-ending story requires a big universe

If your story is going to work, the writer has to choose a scenario that the audience can immerse themselves into over a long period of time. Ideally, you want to create a series than can sustain episodes for several years, such as 'Dallas'.

To do this, you have to create a universe where the characters can all have engaging stories over a long period of time. Additionally, the story arc has to be more than simply the journey between the beginning and end. The story has to provide space for the characters to interact with each other, sometimes making progress toward their goal, sometimes not.

Three dimensional characters

The fact that the story requires the characters to engage the audience, just like real people engage with each other, means that the characters themselves need to be fleshed out into fully realised, three-dimensional people.

What this means in practical terms is that it is vital the audience knows who this person is, where they are going and, almost as importantly, where they are coming from. Fleshing out the character's back-story with the actor's own personal photos, home videos, etc, is a really powerful way to reach out to your audience using real life material.

Contrast this fleshed-out, real character with the action-movie character, who we don't know anything about apart from the fact that he kills bad guys, but who isn't there to develop a connection with the audience. On the other hand, characters in Transmedia projects, if they are to be successful, have to come to life and actually live alongside the viewer in an emotionally real and connected way.

Small casts work better

Bear in mind also that the ensemble cast is more difficult to treat comprehensively in Transmedia. One of the strengths of Transmedia is that it allows the viewer to focus more closely on the individuals. By trying to deal comprehensively with a large cast, you can not only dilute this intimacy but also make it too difficult for the viewer to acquire any kind of meaningful overview of the cast of characters. This is something that should be borne in mind when developing a cast, but can be offset with a decision to just focus on one or two central characters in the story world.

We did this in Flatmates, where we had three main characters, but encouraged the viewers to follow just one character out of this cast. It wasn't necessary for them to follow everyone, just their chosen favourite character. In this case, it had the added benefit of adding to the drama and heightening the sense of competition between the cast members. It was a good example of where the close connection between a character and the viewer provided the type of ongoing audience engagement that helped sustain the show.

Contemporary is easier

If we have a story that is set today, it can often be easier to realise the narrative across Transmedia than it would be with a story set five hundred years ago. Remember, you have to engage the audience in such a way that they suspend their disbelief. It's important to bear in mind, though, that you shouldn't make it too hard for the viewer to do this. For instance, a costume drama from the seventeenth century creates difficulties regarding the integration of new media, e.g. how do you engage the audience with a facebook profile of a seventeenth-century character, a time when the internet wasn't invented yet?

Remember how close you are to the viewer

Every person has a bubble surrounding them that encompasses their personal space. Within this bubble is the viewer's personal space and existence, and outside it is the world they perceive. This is important to remember because, by using personal tools, like email, social media and SMS to connect the viewer to the characters and story, you are in fact entering the viewer's personal space. You are going into their personal bubble.

Consequently, you should be aware that some content can be very difficult for a viewer to deal with if it impacts at such close quarters. For instance, a rape scene would be extremely uncomfortable, but acceptable, viewing on television. I say this because, on television, this type of hard-hitting content is observed by the viewer at a physical and emotional distance. The same content, however, would likely be intolerable for the viewer if carried on a mobile phone because it is very intimate and personal media.

Be careful with Comedy

Comedy on the internet is obviously very popular. It is entertaining for the viewer and just a three-minute laugh can engage the audience in a simple way. It is also accessible anywhere on Youtube, and if you want to laugh at something you can access humorous material quite easily.

You will notice that most of this comedy is not character-driven; rather, it is sketch-driven and therefore you don't have to connect with the characters in order to have a laugh. In drama, on the other hand, it is crucial that the audience has an empathetic connection with the characters.

The level of engagement with comedy is actually quite ephemeral and once consumed people will move on from it. The point is that this transitory engagement makes it quite difficult for a comedy-based product to connect with an audience using Transmedia.

If a story is not character-driven, it won't have the legs to grow. If it doesn't grow, it will run out steam and the audience will abandon it. The trick to comedy is to have central, three-dimensional characters (such as Seinfeld, The Simpsons, The Office). Comedy can be easy to produce over a short period of time. However, the key thing to remember is that the successful comedy genre will follow the rules of drama by creating strong characters while also developing their story-world.

Write it up

When you have addressed the basic ideas and parameters of your idea, you should be in a position to focus yourself on exactly what your story is, what its basic aims are and what you want the characters to achieve. This isn't a very long document, more often it's a one-page synopsis. What it will do is focus the narrative and give the first outline or structure to your Transmedia product.

Chapter III
Development of a Transmedia Bible

Development of a Transmedia Bible

By this stage of the process, you should have a good idea of the type of story you have, what you're going to do, and which media you hope to use. But before you go any further, it's wise at this stage to take a long look at your basic idea. You need now to think through exactly what your idea is. What premise is it built on? What are the rules of the story?

In fact, you're going to have to take that one-page story idea that you've developed and flesh out its characters, narrative, concept and construction into what we'll call our 'Transmedia bible'. This bible will literally set down the rules and parameters of the entire universe that your story exists in. Once you've actually designed this story universe, you will want to be able to show an investor or partner how it works in practice. For this, you will need a visual prototype to convince the funders to part with their money and finance your production.

Okay, I admit 'bible' may be the best descriptive term for this, but it does make it sound a little overwhelming. What we want to do here is break it down and take a look at it in its more manageable component form.

The premise

Your story must be based on a premise and your bible must state clearly what this is. So, at the beginning of this process you must lay down a synopsis of your story. This typically is a clear and succinct summation of the premise. For example, Sofia's Diary would involve a fifteen year old girl who talks about her life, shares her thoughts about the dilemmas she faces and uses new media (such as email and mobile phones) to ask the audience for advice. The idea is that anyone reading the premise will immediately know what the core concept of the story is.

The world of your story

The next thing you have to define is the world that your story inhabits and then lay down the rules which will define that world.

One of the first issues to address is exactly when and where your story is occurring. You have to make it clear if this is a current story happening in England today, or perhaps it is in New York ten, fifty, one hundred years ago or, alternatively, some point in the future or even on an entirely different planet.

The time-framing of your story will, of course, have a profound impact on the world you have to set out here. Remember, if it isn't contemporary then it will require careful and detailed research. For example, if the story is set in the seventeenth century, you will need to know the events and cultural aspects of this period that are influencing your story. It may be obvious to you, the writer, when this story is occurring, but the bible is the 'go-to' for other people to understand your story. Therefore, it's important that it answers as many possible questions they may have.

Bearing this in mind, you have to make sure that the constraints of your time frame are clear and explicit. If your story is grounded in a contemporary time frame and is set in a familiar location, you can assume a greater pre-existing knowledge on the reader's behalf than if you were producing a sci-fi story set on a different planet. In this latter case, you have to set out how the rules of your sci-fi world are different from this world. For instance, have they their own language and, if so, how do you intend to deal with that?

The tone of your story

Basically, your bible will provide you with your plan, setting out the limits beyond which the audience will cease to understand what is happening. Importantly for Transmedia, if you're to maintain a consistency across all your media, all elements of that narrative must occur within the rules that you lay down in your bible. For example, say you are making a story that is aimed primarily at teenagers; you might want to make it explicit in your bible that anything with a sexual or violent tone should not to be used on any platform. We had to tackle this question of tone many times in Sofia's Diary, where we had to decide where we would draw the line at sexual content. We couldn't make it so childish as to be unbelievable, but likewise we didn't want the show to be inappropriate for its younger audience.

Whatever you decide about tone, it is important that it is consistently maintained across all media. Also bear in mind that, in the future, when someone perhaps goes to make a feature film of your tweenie story, this content/tone rule has to be complied with, otherwise it would confuse the audience by undermining the expectations for the entire brand.

Define the characters

Having provided all the background to your story, you will now need to turn to your characters and set about defining them. You will have to provide insights into who they are, what they like/dislike, what motivates them and what they want to achieve. In many ways it is a similar process to creating a script for television. The important distinction here, though, is that you have to be more expansive in your view because you are not just writing about how this character will appear on television. Remember, this is also where the video, books, web, blogs, etc, will all derive their basis for existence.

The danger is that you will be tempted to focus on one output when defining what you want them to achieve. Most producers are used to creating a story for one media, say for a 45-minute television script. These, quite typical, constraints mean that you don't have to flesh out aspects of the characters that you won't be able to display on screen. Bear in mind that, for Transmedia, you have to create the features for your characters as they appear across all media.

The lesson is that you will have to be expansive in your view of the people you are creating, not defining them solely in terms of one particular platform. One thing you don't have to worry too much about is providing the absolute last word on the total number of characters you intend to use. Describing the initial cast of characters doesn't mean you can't add other characters at a later stage.

In these types of projects, you have to remember the ways in which people connect with other people. They connect with them because they are engaged with them in an emotional sense and will want to know more about them. Following on from this, because the notion of the audience character connection is so important to Transmedia, consequently the definition and the richness of your characters will determine a lot about how and why your audience connects with your product.

Define your world

In terms of stories set in the past, you will need to set out the parameters of your world. This is helpful to the reader of your bible, as they will need to gain an accurate sense of the limits of what can be done and achieved in your story-world.

To do this, you can perhaps include Wiki-links on your bible, which can provide you with ready-made (and useful) tools that can help you define your story and give it its correct historical context. Another benefit of using Wiki-links is that you don't have to write the entire geography of a place or the history of the period into your bible. At the same time, by using these links you are providing the reader of the bible with a user-friendly means of identifying the geographical, historical or cultural realities that your story is operating within. A good rule to remember here is that, while most stories need a contextual frame to define them, you don't have to invent every detail of that frame.

For instance, for historical stories (and even contemporary ones), real life history provides a ready-made frame that you can use to create context. If it is an historical story, your bible could include a timeline of relevant historical events from the time before and after your story occurs. This would be very helpful to frame the story in a sequence of events and lays down quite clearly what reality the story and characters have to live within.

What you want to achieve, within this part of the bible, is a type of instructive clarity that should be easy for anyone to comprehend. At this stage, you will want the bible-user to have a clear understanding of the story and, where relevant, know its historical, social and geographical contexts. I should also mention that it can very useful, where possible, to include a visual element that can capture one or more of these contexts and communicate their meaning directly.

More than this, you will want the bible-user to have a clear sense of how these contexts impact on and contain the story. Remember, when the bible has been written (either by yourself or a hired writer), an investor, broadcast partner, producer, director, or writer will need to be able to pick up your bible and know exactly what you intend the bible to convey, and specifically know what the characters can and can't do within your story.

For example, if your story is taking place in Fiji in the nineteenth century, you might want to provide a historical context by including a timeline of Fijian history in this period. You might want to provide geographical context by pointing out Fiji is an island in the Pacific Ocean and further stating it is a tropical island, etc. This provides the broad definitions within which your story is played out.

Alternatively, the historical context need not be concerned with high school history lessons. For example, if your story is about a computer hacker in the 1980s you might want to include information about the origins of computer hacking, e.g. was the internet available? Or perhaps describe the types of technology then available, and what developments have taken place subsequently.

What is important in your vision is that you are clear and as detailed as necessary to instruct the user about what your vision actually is. This is vital because consistency across all platforms is vital for Transmedia. It is vital because someone later will read this bible and need to be able to visualise the entire historical and visual scenario and apply it in an even fashion across all media.

Timeline

A clear sense of the time-span of the story is necessary to define the plot. To achieve the desired clarity at this early stage of development, you will have to set out in some detail the story timeline. The timeline will, as the term suggests, define in the first instance the period of time that the story spans, be it ten weeks, ten months or ten years.

Other information on the timeline will include the time a specific character exists in the story. This information will clearly show the time a character is born or moves into the area. It will also include the time a character's involvement with the story terminates and perhaps include the information showing that the character has died or simply moved away.

The other key information included on the timeline is when specific plotlines occur. These plotlines in themselves will set out when they begin and end, and will also demonstrate what characters are involved in the plot. Naturally, all these plots occur within the overall frame of the story timeline.

The plot

Having defined the premise of the story, defined your characters and placed them in the world they inhabit, you can outline what the initial plot in your drama involves.

As previously mentioned, the plot will occur on that defined part of the timeline where the drama and key character interactions occur. The plot outline will involve you defining the story in terms of where it starts, what is the drama, the conflict, the mission or objective. It is the important and recurring undercurrent that makes the audience return to your show again and again.

For instance, the plot of the 1980s television series 'Moonlighting' revolved around the love interest between Bruce Willis and Cybill Sheperd. The romantic tension between these two detectives remained the basic plot concept for the entire series. Moonlighting was a ratings winner for three out of four of its seasons; however, once the producers abandoned the core tension and Bruce and Cybill became a couple, the audience abandoned the show. In this instance, once the writers removed the central plot pillar that was supporting the show, the basis for the audience watching it collapsed.

Years later, maybe the writers of the television series 'Bones' were aware of this fact. Currently, the series is in its fifth season, but has retained the same plot that rests on the tension between the two leading characters. This key plot tension remains unresolved and thereby keeps the audience returning to watch the relationship develop.

Dressing your bible

Having created your bible, it is important to present it as visually interesting as possible. You need to take your text and, at every opportunity, transfer it into an illustrated document. When using photographs, mind-maps, illustrations, and maps of the world you are creating, you need to keep this as visual as possible. Remember, this is primarily a communication document and the more you clearly illustrate your vision, the better the reader will grasp what you want to achieve.

Using the bible

Once again, it is this bible that will shape all your outputs, whether they are comic books, games, books, a television series, radio programmes or whatever.

In order to create any of these outputs, you will have to refer to the bible to find out about a particular character, location, or plotline to ensure it doesn't play against the rules of your world. Instead, all of these outputs should act like windows to the world you have created.

Bear in mind that other producers you will partner with for specific productions will also need to know what they can and can't do in terms of story, character and the applicable outputs. To do this, they will use your bible.

Also, it's important to remember that your bible will evolve over time as you add new characters and tweak the plot. However, while this process will allow you to further develop your content, it cannot go so far as to contradict the basic rules of your story that have already been broadcast. This makes sense as, if something has been broadcast and it has been established as part of the basic rules and history of the story, it cannot be easily unpicked. To do so could undermine the overall credibility of the story in the minds of the audience. Telling that a full season was just a character's dream doesn't work anymore.

Some advice on different media

I now want to outline how you can expand your bible to include some of the different outputs for your story. This stage is important in Transmedia, as you will need to decide how to create concepts for these media out of your original story.

The book of your story

The novel is a perennial favourite and can be an inexpensive way to gain a foothold in the mainstream media. The central character or characters typically will have strong parts to play in any book as they require a greater level of depth of writing than other elements.

Again, it need not focus on the entire narrative, but be a self-contained story that doesn't require support from other media and doesn't impinge on other parts of the overall narrative. That is not, of course, to say that it can act independently of the other outputs; like all Transmedia elements, it has to be complementary to, and definitely not contradict, the overall story. We will discuss how to deal with publishing issues in a later chapter.

Comic books

The comic book is a medium that has again become very popular. Take, for example, the number of Hollywood movies that are based on comic books; this is proof both of the resurgence of the comic book medium and how it transfers over to other platforms. Likewise, many film and television producers are creating comic books out of their existing productions.

One of the reasons for this growth is that creating a comic book is an easy and inexpensive way to establish ownership of your story. Hiring an artist to create your comic book and release it as an e-book will cost you between €2,000 and 5,000.

Because it can represent your overall story in a very accessible way, you can use it in a variety of ways to explain to partners and investors what your product is about. Again and again I have found the simplicity of the comic book as a visual aide extremely useful to communicate with investors, in a very simple way, what a story and its world is about. With this in mind, if your story is suitable for comic book representation I would opt for it early on in the development process.

Casual games

Another area that is becoming extremely popular is the casual game. I am not talking about multi-million dollar console games that require a lot of time on the user's part; even if you eventually want to create a console game, the type of budget and partnership required here will come later in the development process. Initially, however, it is quite possible to develop casual games which typically are the simple games and puzzles that you find on your mobile phone. For some people with a background in the computer games world, you can go ahead and develop a casual game using your own resources.

Radio

Radio is a great way to launch your story. The type of radio show can take a variety of forms, ranging from radio soaps to a radio column or radio sketch show.

We initially launched Sofia's Diary as a radio drama and, to encourage interaction with the audience, we looked for advice for Sofia from her audience. This worked well for a time, but then the audience also began seek Sofia's advice for their own issues and problems. So, on the back of this demand, we also produced a radio advice show that dealt with Sofia's response to her fans' own personal issues.

The Web

This can include the website, character blogs, Facebook sites and Twitter pages. The crucial thing to remember here is that the site, once launched, will involve an ongoing investment. You have to work out how you are going to manage the content and update it frequently which, of course, involves costs incurred by writers, editors and the like.

As you develop a comprehensive web presence you may also want to establish other pages linked to your website. For instance, you may want Twitter alerts for your characters, Facebook fan pages, Facebook pages for the characters, or start discussion forums.

All of these are really useful in engaging your audience. However, you should be aware that these types of ancillary web pages all require ongoing proper moderation to encourage content, edit comments and eliminate spam. This is especially the case in web forums, which need a lot of management and time investment if they are to work properly.

Mobile Apps

Another group of products that are becoming increasingly popular are mobile phone apps. These may include apps for iPhones, Blackberries, Android phones or any other mobile devices that exist. The free games app in this scenario is an efficient promotional tool for new users to access your web content. These apps can be free to the user, which provides you with an even more attractive marketing tool.

However, if you already have a community, you can monetise their existing interest in your product by developing an app, and then selling it for revenue. I would say that it is probably best to start by issuing apps for free to increase your public profile; then, once you're established, progress to selling the content in the form of mobile games or exclusive story content (e.g. characters' photographs, videos, or even their private thoughts).

If you successfully market apps to your fans, because of the endless number of possible apps that can be created, you will create an endless revenue source for your story.

Web series

At this point, once you have developed your website, you can test the potential of your audiovisual content by creating a web series. The web series is not as expensive an undertaking as a television production. However, compared to all the other media we have mentioned here, to produce your web series will require the biggest budget yet.

I will say that, regardless of the greater expense, it has shown itself to be a very valuable tool when used as a prequel for a story, to develop a character or set out the basis for a plot.

Television

The great advantage of the television show is that it simultaneously unites your audience and massively boosts your credibility. You cannot underestimate the benefit gained when it comes to selling your apps, DVDs, books or comics. What is also important is that it may not even be the main vehicle for your storyline. What I mean by this is that having Sofia's Diary on television wasn't crucially important for our core demographic, who had initially accessed us online, and who continued to access the content in that way. However, for us to sell products, we had to feature on the radars of the mothers, grandparents, aunts and uncles if they were to buy the books, pyjamas, games, etc.

If we were outside the television, not only would they have not known about us, but they wouldn't have taken us seriously. It is still the case that television provides a validation that the solely internet phenomenon cannot (yet) match in the eyes of the consumer.

Live Shows

A number of television shows are currently being transferred into the live show format, many in the musical format. So this can be something you can think about. Can your product be transferred into a show, a play, or even a monologue? If it can, this can be an effective way to raise awareness of your product, gain direct contact with your audience and also increase credibility.

If you can do some cross-marketing with your other media, it can be an effective revenue generator. It can also be a good way into, perhaps, producing a DVD of your story by recording a live event and then selling it.

The Feature Film

The same logic that underpins the continuing importance of television also reaffirms the dominance of the feature film, in the hierarchy of all this. When it comes to monetising your story, the feature film is the Holy Grail of what you want to achieve. It's an extremely expensive enterprise and only if you're very lucky will you get a studio to finance it all. The advantages are that you get to potentially tap the global market. At the same time, the success needn't necessarily be global in scope, even if it's a local film, way more people will hear about a film than will eventually see it, as a movie creates a buzz way beyond its reach.

Remember, no other entertainment product has a bigger advertising budget than the feature film. Even a local film can have a marketing budget way beyond what a television show can command. Don't forget that even if your feature film loses money, this type of a loss leader maybe be important to augment the credibility of your brand and can even be recouped elsewhere, particularly in licensing.

Licensing

The licensing world, whether it be for games, clothes or fast food toys, means that you can make more money on these type of products than even from a successful movie. Nine times out of ten, the real money from a feature film endeavour comes through the licensing agreements. Of course, these types of deals don't just fall out of the sky as the licensing professionals will only consider a deal with you if you have a strong track record and a very high public presence. They not only need to know your show will have the level of exposure necessary to drive sales, but that it possesses the longevity to sustain them. (This isn't something that you will typically be involved with at an early stage of production, and I will go into this in detail in a special chapter devoted to licensing later in the book).

Getting started with your prototype

Bear in mind that, when you develop your idea and flesh out what media you are going to use, the next step should be to bring your production to the finance stage. However, unless you are an Hollywood major, you most likely won't have the financial firepower to develop and launch across all the media from the start. In other words, you are going to have to demonstrate to your investors how this product will appear when it is launched.

Developing a product example for each platform would be prohibitively expensive at this point. What you need to focus on is what is available to you in order to best demonstrate how your product works on one, or maybe two, platforms. Essentially, you need a 'live', functioning example of your product. You need a prototype.

When getting started with your prototype product, I would recommend that you focus on those media that you are most familiar with. Launch on a medium you are most comfortable with and break out from there. For instance, if you're a web-based company you might want to initially focus on the internet, because this is what you know and this is what you do well with. So, in this instance, you might want to create a game first. If you are a television-oriented company, you might want to produce your short form episode or a pilot for the internet. Again, if you are more familiar with the publishing world, maybe your starting point is books, or perhaps writing articles for magazines. Remember, you shouldn't try to do this all at once, but plan and timeline your expected expansion into other media.

The move into different media

It's important that your expansion timeline includes not just the list of media you intend to expand into. You need also to have a synopsis of what these next media will achieve - for example, if it is a comic book you may have some illustrations and text to convey what it is about. For a television series, for instance, you might have a synopsis of what it should contain; if it's a video game, you should have visual representations of what you see as final product.

This timeline will also be crucial further down the line, when you go to convince funders and partners to invest in your product. It is vital that they be able to conceptualise the future growth in the business and see the future stages of expansion (more about this later in the book).

Another thing to remember here is that, with Transmedia, expansion into new outputs and new visualisations of your story creates more opportunities. The benefits of having 'live' examples of your story can be seen not just at this early stage of development but throughout the lifetime of your product. For instance, I found what was important in selling Sofia's Diary internationally was the fact they it had already been deployed in a territory. Because of this, when I was going to meetings to talk about Sofia's Diary expanding into a new country, I would always bring as many visual examples of the product as I could (be they videos clips, magazines or perhaps books). Obviously, this was invaluable when I was in meetings pitching a story that was not just an idea but was a proven successful product. One of the things I learned is that, although the world is full of ideas, real products are fewer in existence and consequently more in demand.

Your story, your property

A really important part of your launching your story at this point is to establish ownership and authorship of your work. If you pick your Transmedia world and, without any deployment, you go to a funder and tell them about your great idea, you are leaving yourself wide open to a number of dangerous pitfalls.

For starters, if you have nothing but an idea, it's possible that an investor or partner will likely make some claim on ownership of the idea in return for investment. In the worst case scenario, they could rip your idea off. Ripping off an idea is a lot more difficult if you have already created a public presence for that story in the media.

Therefore, it is vital, if you have any resources, to make the first deployment yourself and thereby establishing authorship yourself. Later, when you go looking for funds, you'll know the story exists and you own it. By launching your prototype yourself (be it, say, a comic book, web series or blog), you may have built a community which makes the product even more valuable while, at the same time, reinforcing your ownership of your intellectual property.

Expansion

At this point you may have one or two active outputs for your story, perhaps on radio and an online game in motion or a webseries. So, having established maybe a modest public presence for your story, it might be time to take things up a gear or two and really start to expand the profile and outputs for your story. Therefore, you need to follow a clearly laid-out expansion timeline that identifies what your next output should be, and also which media you want to expand into in year one, year two and so on.

Chapter IV
Funding Your Transmedia Project

- So now you need money
- Early stages finance
- Spending plans
- Taking It up a gear, going mainstream
- The Presentation

Funding Your Transmedia Project

So now you need money

At this stage of your development, you have a product and you have a plan. What you need now is the money to finance what you want to achieve, and unless you've deep pockets you need to persuade other people to give you the money.

Now, pretty much like other business finance operations, the ease with which you are going to get this cash will depend, in the first instance, on whether you have an established business reputation, connections and a proven track record. In this case, you have already shown that you're not a high risk venture and, provided you have a good plan and product, you're chances of getting finance are pretty good.

But what if you're just starting out and have a great plan and product but have no track record? In this scenario, you have an obvious problem as the fact is we live in a world where there is more content on offer than there is demand for that content. Therefore, you've got to really think outside the box if you want to get financed.

The good news is that, as we've seen in Chapter II, the web and social media allows you to get exposure to incubate your project and get it established. It allows you to create your project and, using seed money, give life to it before you have to look for serious finance. The fact that you will have a live, working story - be it in book, blog, webseries or comic book form - will be a big asset to you when you are approaching financiers and investors. Before you approach anyone though, you might want to take some time to identify who the likely backers of your project will be.

Early stages finance

The first thing I would advise people when looking to finance a Transmedia operation is to check and see what the local enterprise bodies and agencies have to offer in the way of loan or grants for your project. In a post-recession or recovery climate you might be surprised at how much the government still has to offer your business in hard cash terms, especially in the areas of IT, games and digital content.

For instance, in many Western countries there are still numerous government agencies giving grants and small loans to start-up companies and micro-businesses, especially the ones that are working within the new media. You will often find the government has identified new media as a future growth industry and accordingly they are anxious to support start-ups in this area. Therefore, when you go to apply for a grant or loan you should market your company as a new media company and less as a vehicle for television or film.

The pitfall that many companies often fall into is that they go to a government business agency looking for a loan or grant and start talking about their great ideas for a television programme or feature film. Often in these cases, the company will be immediately redirected to their local film board or broadcaster to develop their great idea while missing a great opportunity to acquire finance for their business. It's important, therefore, that whatever agency you are in negotiations with don't see you as just another person with a good idea for a movie or television show.

Instead, you will want to project yourself as a new-media company with long-term business strategies and goals. In this vein, it is vital for you to develop your media company profile and recast your creative products and ideas into business proposals; these proposals should clearly identify how they would create jobs that will add to the industry as a whole. It may also advance your case if you are in a position to talk to the agency about any innovation or research you are undertaking. Essentially, it is about re-phrasing or recasting your plan in such a way that it engages with the agency's own priorities and aims.

In practical terms, when you go to these meetings take care to be to be focused on your business plan (identifying specifics including timelines, the business needs and, of course, the return on the investment). Importantly, you shouldn't dilute your business-centric approach by talking about your synopsis, cool graphics and exciting story scripts, no matter how proud of them you happen to be! These government business grants can be significant in their scale, ranging from tens of thousands of euros to hundreds of thousands. Vitally, they will allow you to start your company or, if you are already in operation, to hire people to grow and develop the project.

Other funding options available for this early incubation and development phase of your project are the short-term funding grants issued by regional film bodies. These regional film bodies frequently have grants specifically tailored for new media which can make your application quite straightforward. However, you can also apply for funding for a short film based on your Transmedia world. This short film can be used as a pilot or prototype of what your product can be. This can be an especially useful type of short-term funding for start-up companies.

The Media Programme also represents an alternative avenue for you to pursue. This programme provides development grants of up to €60,000 for one-off documentary or fiction projects. Alternatively, you could apply for one of the grants that have become available in the last few years for interactive projects. Under this scheme, grants are available of up to €150,000. This type of grant obviously has enormous potential to allow you to develop the interactive tools necessary to incubate your project.

The last option is to ask your friends and family or, alternatively, self-fund this stage of the project. I don't just say this as an afterthought; originally, when we were pitching Sofia's Diary for funding, we were collecting dozens of rejection letters. So we started by self-funding all the elements in the early stages until we obtained revenue further down the road. We were able to do this as a company that was already up and running, as we cut money from services and diverted other revenues into the Sofia's Diary project.

Spending plans

Once you have raised the money, you need to know where you are going to spend it. One of the first things you will do is to hire a writer to write your scripts and produce the content for your different elements, be they your game, blog or web-series. This is the seed finance phase of your project and your spending at this point will, of course, depend on how you want to prioritise and what you need to achieve in the early development stages.

A typical early spend is on website set-up and design. You may also want to develop a mobile game. Or, depending again on your priorities, you may need to produce a pilot episode or a series of five or six webisodes to get traction; thereafter, you would use it for promotional purposes to demonstrate what you want to achieve with your product and what your overall vision is.

You may also want to hire a digital marketing person or company to undertake social media marketing. If you want to avoid these spends, you will have to invest your own time and research on how to market your product on social media networks. You may start this process knowing how to use the medium, but you will probably need to put in a great deal of time and effort to find out how to promote and market your content on the internet. From my own experience, I wouldn't underestimate the amount of knowledge that is needed in this area. For instance, you will have to learn how to negotiate links with other websites and how to increase search engine results to optimise your appearance on random searches.

You might also have to create a Facebook application and then hire someone to create content for your Facebook pages. You may need someone to write character blogs, create and moderate an online forum and finally manage all the information appearing on your sites online. This person has to produce your online content, manage and promote the face of your product and then promote communication with your community. You have to appreciate that this is, in itself, a full-time job for at least one person if you want the company to grow.

As you work through this crucial incubation and development stage you will continually have to focus on acquiring traction with your audience, often simply to prove you can acquire an audience. Acquiring audience traction and quantifying your community is often vital to your product's ongoing existence. I say this because if you can't get audience traction now you will find it very difficult to persuade later investors that you will ever get it. You cannot be passive about this and simply believe 'if we build it (the website) they (the audience) will come' - because quite often they don't!

One of the most efficient ways you can acquire this vital audience traction is to partner with someone who already has a community and who can promote your content. Ideally, you should approach a company that will benefit from your content so they may be more amenable to your pitch. However, if you are a start-up company, though it might be tempting to put in a call to the companies with the biggest, busiest websites, it may prove disappointing. Approaching a big company and asking them to carry your content on their website is less likely to yield positive results; since you have no track record, you are less likely to be green-lighted. Again, this is an occasion where you could set your sights on a local newspaper or radio station website where, despite your lack of track record, they may be more amenable to your idea. Another point to remember is that, as your product isn't fully developed yet, it may still have elements that don't quite work. If this is the case, you may perhaps be better advised to develop and correct your product on a site which doesn't expose its weaknesses to a wider audience.

To sum up where you should be at this stage, basically you want to have created something that has an audience that is quantifiable in numbers, something that exists with an ongoing and continuous audience traction that can be taken seriously by partners and investors. Once you have achieved this, you are ready to take it up a gear and compete in the mainstream.

Taking it up a gear, going mainstream

Now that you have incubated your content online and garnered a small to medium-sized community, or if you already have a track record, you will want to move up to the next stage of development. What you need to do now is deploy your project nationally or internationally. In order to do this, you will have to acquire far greater funding to match your increased aspirations. There are a number of different routes available to you:

1. Government agencies - national and regional
As we mentioned earlier, there are still plenty of grants available, despite governments implementing spending cuts. Canada is leading the way in this type of funding, with generous grants still available at Federal and Provincial levels, but there is a variety of film and television grants also available in many other countries (see Appendix).

2. Broadcasters
In the first instance, if there is a television element in your project, broadcasters are the obvious primary source of financing and licensing for your content.

Secondly, traditional broadcasters are quite rapidly expanding into the area of web commissions. This involves broadcasters licensing content that originally appeared on the internet. CBS, for instance, commissioned the series '$#*! My Dad Says' starring William Shatner, based on a popular Twitter account.

In the UK, broadcasters have started to commission programmes for their own websites in order to test how the content will work; they will then assess their chances of transferring the series onto mainstream television. These are examples of things commissioned as webseries that, when successfully received, were later broadcast on television. Don't lose sight of the fact that the broadcasters are actually trying to do the very same things as you are. If you don't have the track record to go to television straight away, the broadcaster may be quite willing to help you develop your product for the web and then transfer it onto television. In this way, the broadcaster can often be more in sync with your development timetable throughout the process than most other Transmedia partners. For instance, a partnership with a broadcaster early on makes sense when you are supplying web content, and then continues to be beneficial if you progress and make the move to television

3. Newspapers

The new online presences of the traditional print media can also provide you with another useful source of revenue at this point. One significant example of this growing phenomenon occurred when The New York Times and Rupert Murdoch's News Corporation newspapers recently started charging readers who wish to access their content online.

However, the challenge this type of move presents for news companies is that, if you start charging people for news content sites, the reader will have to get something more than just straight news from them. In other words, because news in itself isn't so exclusive it doesn't in itself draw people onto a specific news site. Consequently, newspaper companies have found that they also have to provide other unique content alongside the traditional news material if they want to encourage people to pay to access their websites.

I think it is pretty safe to predict that, as more newspapers introduce pay to view areas, they will need even more exclusive content to fill them if they want to attract sufficient site traffic. The important point for us here is that this challenge presents a great opportunity for independent production companies to offer this type of exclusive online content to newspapers. The content can include anything from documentaries to entertainment and, I believe, represents a significant potential growth area for online generated revenue.

4. Advertising, product placement and sponsorship

Before we start talking about the specifics of advertising, I just want to outline the differences between the types of agencies that are out there. I say this because there are important differences between advertising agencies, media agencies and PR agencies and you will need to know who amongst them you should approach.

(i) Advertising / Creative Agencies

Advertising agencies are normally concerned with creating the material and content used in television and mainstream marketing campaigns. In the normal course of events, I don't work with them because I am also in the business of producing short-form content and am competing with them in the sense that we are both selling creativity.

(ii) Media Agencies

Normally we find ourselves working with media agencies who are not themselves in the business of creating content. For these companies, your audience is your commodity, as they buy media space in bulk and sell it on to their clients. As long as the proposition makes good business sense (i.e. you are charging the right amount for the chance to access your audience) they will see you as an opportunity.

(iii) PR Agencies

Lastly, there are PR agencies who are principally concerned with the business of preparing press releases and dealing with the mainstream media. They are not usually in the market buying advertising space so we don't normally find ourselves dealing with them. They want to get free exposure for their clients. We do, however, hire them as part of a marketing campaign to promote our content in the mainstream media.

To understand how online advertising currently works, and why it is only slowly changing, we need to understand where the industry is coming from. In many ways, the advertising industry has been one of the slowest areas to adapt to new media and has seemed rooted in their reliance of old media-generated revenue (television, newspapers etc). The big problem for the industry is that, despite the fact that so many consumers spend considerable time online, internet advertising revenues remain relatively small. For example, a typical A/B or C classed person spends on average the same (or more) time online every day as they do watching television.

However, despite this parity in time, they are nowhere near advertising spends. In fact, looking at the advertising spends for television and the internet combined, online advertising represents just 10 per cent of the total figure. It is still a challenge to get advertising revenues here because the industry is still catching up with the fact that the audiences have moved to digital platforms. This can largely be accounted for by the fact that most advertising agencies are still focused on quantity rather than the quality of the contact, i.e. they would much prefer to air an advert in a programme that has a non-segmented million viewers instead of using digital media to target 100,000 people, who comprise their target demographic.

Again, largely because the industry has always focused on bottom-line audience or readership numbers, it hasn't adapted to the shifting audience that exists online. In many ways, it is mirroring the way the music industry was also reluctant to embrace the changes that new media forced upon it.

The problem here for Transmedia is that, if you go along this route, you will be dealing with an advertising industry that has to change but doesn't yet know how they will achieve this. To help navigate this very uncertain sponsorship and advertising world, here are a few tips I've picked up along the way:

(i) They have their own schedules. This means they will only invest when they have a product to launch; therefore, if you want a piece of their advertising budget, you need to adjust your schedule to the sponsor's marketing schedule. Quite simply, if a car company is going to launch their new model in May and you're ready to launch your product in March, you need to delay your start date if you want a slice of their ad money.

Trying to deal with multiple sponsors obviously presents a problem because they all have their own schedules. The multiple schedules of the multiple sponsors isn't necessarily an insurmountable problem; however, as you can in many ways predict, within the peaks and troughs of budget spends will occur. The idea here is that there are seasons when you will have big advertising investments by companies (e.g. third-quarter ahead of Christmas) and other times when companies hold back on spending (e.g. January-February is usually the annual trough for ad spending). Also, be aware of the specific seasonal requirements of individual companies and see if your content might be attractive to the company's target audience. For example, soft drinks companies invest more in marketing at summer time, so they might be interested in investing in your product if you could provide a series of summer themed episodes.

(ii) You need to have connections with agencies to know when campaigns will start. For example, you should be proactive and track down what car companies are launching new models in the next year, and when exactly they are commencing their marketing campaigns. This is important because, when they're unveiling a big product like this, they will have money to spend.

(iii) Remember that, because companies are selling a product (and not art), you have to convince them that your art can sell their product. The best way you can convince them is to show them that you have a quantifiable audience. Accordingly, when you approach them you need a distribution partner (be it portal, newspaper or broadcaster) that demonstrates the fact you have a quantifiable audience watching at a specific time for a specific duration. By providing an advertiser with this type of data, you enable them to see how much they would typically spend reaching this type of audience. Once they know what size audience you can provide, they will know how much they would be willing to spend on buying it. The figure they arrive at will be your advertising revenue. The exception to this rule is the rare prestige partnership that occasionally occurs if you have top talent on your show, e.g. Lexus sponsored a webseries 'Web therapy' because Lisa Kudrow was starring in it. This was attractive to Lexus, not because it would necessarily attract a big audience, but because it gained publicity from the surrounding media and PR buzz surrounding the web project.

(iv) Throughout my own engagement with advertisers, it has been key not just to concentrate on what we can offer online in terms of audience, but also do a lot of PR. This is partly because of the industry mistrust of online media. For instance, if an account manager uses a television advertising agency he won't be blamed if it doesn't produce results because he has applied a tried and tested industry formula. Accordingly, if the product didn't sell, it wouldn't be seen as his fault. On the other hand, if he invests a small amount in a webseries that doesn't work he may get into trouble because it is viewed as a risky venture.

Accordingly, because of the perceived level of risk involved in online advertising spends, we have to show that we can do more than just deliver an audience. In Sofia's Diary, for example, when we signed up our sponsors online we decided not to charge them when we got television exposure. In this way, they got a far greater return for their initial agreement. For us we created valuable goodwill towards the product and subsequent projects. We gave this extra return to our sponsors in a different way in 'Flatmates'. On that occasion, Ford were sponsoring the show and, when we undertook a national casting process, we did go the extra mile by doing the various press interviews in a Ford car which, in turn, appeared in newspapers nationwide.

5 . Tax credits

Tax credits are widely available for television and film production. Ireland is one country that takes a generous view of film and television funding. This is especially so if your project has a television element with a tax credit available of up to 28 per cent of your budget. This is one of the few tax credits available in the world for audiovisual content as it is usually only available for film content.

There are a few other countries (including the UK) that allow tax credits for feature films and some others that have credits aimed at many more Transmedia products, like Canada that provides tax credits for feature films, television and new media. Don't underestimate the benefits of this type of icentives regime as it can represent up to 40 per cent of your budget, making it a hugely valuable part of your business plan.

6. Private equity and private investors

For this type of investment, you need to highlight the digital media side of your plan if you wish to attract investors. It is a fact that these investors are usually focused on IT and software companies. Accordingly, for many private equity investors, companies that are developing software and mobile phone technologies may have a better return on investment than entertainment products. For Transmedia companies, therefore, an emphasis on new media aspects of your plan will help you break through this quite normal institutional bias. There are also many countries (e.g. Ireland, UK) that provide tax credits to companies who wish to invest in start-up enterprises. These provide a favourable climate for you to attract private investment. One important thing to note here is the fact that many companies are attracted to media investment by the difficult to quantify prestige factor. Investing in a media company offers opportunities to get involved in the media industry that may not otherwise present themselves. By balancing this aspect of your profile with strong IT/new media credentials, you are providing a sound business incentive to support the former, more emotional, attraction. This type of mix can be invaluable when you come to present your product to potential investors.

The Presentation

For the presentation you need to book the meeting and you need to bring three things:

1. Visual.   2. Visual.   3. Visual.

I am continually amazed how, in this audiovisual industry, most presentations are still based on black and white text. When you're talking to broadcasters or newspaper editors, remember that texts can be visualised in many different ways. For example, by making and presenting a pilot episode. Comic books are also fantastic when it comes to visualising and selling. Ultimately, what you should aim to do is to try and create as many elements as you can that show how you plan to develop your overall plan. Remember, by showing a timeline of visual content makes your plan easy to understand and ensures that everyone is on the same page.

Another important thing to remember is, if you are going to meet with a big broadcasting company or media group, you should first establish ownership of your product. If you have followed the advice outlined here and incubated your content on the web on as a novel, you have already established ownership. Quite simply, because you've done this, they can't steal your idea. Also, they won't be able to say they want 50 per cent of the rights because, if your product is 'live', you are bringing more to the table than just an idea. In essence, you are bringing a product, an audience and sufficient proof that you may succeed long-term.

It is also quite important that you bring a business timeline to the investors. If you want to have a long-term relationship with these partners/investors then you need a plan that demonstrates a lot of thought has been put into where you currently are in the development of your product, where the product is playing, what audience you have and, most importantly, where it is going (including the future platforms you intend to expand into). The last point is, of course, what investors want to see.

Investors need to be convinced that your product is not just a one-off but is part of a comprehensive, long-term plan to succeed. This multi-layered plan also offsets a bias that often operates against entertainment projects when they appear to be one-shot investments. Investors are often wary of putting their money in entertainment projects, such as movies, as the perception is that they are one-shot projects that will likely lose money. To tackle this prejudice, by emphasising for instance the web content, apps revenue or licensing potential, you can demonstrate the benefits of the multi-platform Transmedia approach over traditional media investment opportunities.

Chapter V
Writing for Transmedia

Writing for Transmedia

Having written the bible, developed your story-world and gained the necessary funding, it is now time to focus on creating and writing for the various outputs of the story.

Until I sat down to write Sofia's Diary, I had no real scriptwriting experience, let alone Transmedia writing experience. I had published a few articles and a few books, but they were IT (Information Technology) based books. I had no experience of novel or scriptwriting.

For me, it was always going to be a process of trial and error. As if this wasn't daunting enough, I was learning the basics of scriptwriting at a time when there were no rules for writing for Transmedia. Looking back now, I can say that myself and my co-writer partner, Marta Gomes, had a lot of freedom in the process; a lot of freedom to learn, but freedom also to write what we thought would work on this new media. We had no bible, no recognised format, and no guide (like the guide you would have, say, if you were writing a three-act play or a short story).

It's fair to say, I suppose, we were literally making it up as we were going along. We had one key tool in this learning process. Because Sofia's Diary had a large interactive element, we were day by day discovering what worked in Transmedia writing, based on the users' feedback. If something didn't work, the audience either complained or, worse, was unresponsive. Strong audience engagement and positive feedback were also, of course, helpful for us on this steep learning curve.

Goals and objectives

We are living in a time when the old monolithic media are fragmenting, audiences are becoming more specialised and the ways in which you can access content are becoming more diverse. All these factors mean it is way harder to reach a large audience with one stream of content played out on one single medium. It is also making this traditional one-content, one-medium model less and less profitable. This, therefore, creates challenges and puts into focus what our aim should be when we are developing a Transmedia brand. Therefore, if I had to define our objective, I would say the goal of Transmedia writing is to develop a long-running series that is made specifically for a number of different media.

Taking a closer look at this, like most other media producers I wanted to create a long-running series. 'Dallas', 'ER' or 'CSI' are examples of a successful long-running series and, in terms of longevity, they are what you are aiming for. The obvious benefit of this type of success is that you are gaining a sustained revenue stream.

With Transmedia, however, it's important to remember that if you are going to achieve long-term success you have to plan long-term. What this means is that when you are developing ideas you have to map out exactly the type of platforms that are going to sustain the product for a long time. So, if you are going to have a long-running series, you really need to plan when you are going to expand and what media you are going to expand into.

For instance, when we were starting to develop Sofia's Diary, we had to plan a process that saw the show break into various media at various stages of its success. We didn't have a big studio budget, but at the same time we didn't just want to create a web series. Although we started out with content on the web, via mobile phones and through a magazine column, we also had to plan initially to have a radio show attached and add video content at a later stage. As the show developed we would consider additional platforms and games applications as we convinced other partners to get involved.

Another key point here is that this type of growth allowed us to stay in control of our brand and the direction at a time when a partnership with a bigger business would have been a one-sided arrangement. It would necessarily have been one-sided because, at that time, we didn't have the expertise or track record to bolster our credibility. So in many ways the internet allowed us to keep control; for instance, it allowed us as a small company to create our own entertainment franchise without having to compromise our creative process.

It also meant that we kept full ownership of the product because we didn't have to share our intellectual property with, say, a broadcaster or publisher. It also meant that we didn't have to engage in the often fruitless battle of getting past old media gatekeepers to have our content broadcast or published. Instead, we controlled the distribution of our content and built our brand. In short, it provided us with the space to grow on our terms and develop our own unique story.

The showrunner

In order to realise your vision, you have to be pretty clear about who exactly is running the show. I discovered early on that, because of all the collaborative elements of creating a show, you need ultimately one person to unify all the elements and push forward your plan. The showrunner in a US television series literally runs the show - he is the head writer, the big director who leads the writing team and controls the output.

The showrunner in Transmedia does pretty much the same thing, only more. Practically speaking, the showrunner needs to know what they want to achieve throughout the different platforms (not just television) and also unite a team of blog writers, game writers, or scriptwriters to achieve a unified voice. He is the arbiter of the voice, the person who creates the consistency of the show in terms of storyline and across all the media platforms. This is an especially difficult task for Transmedia, where you have to create a voice that is consistent among a group of people that often work in different places and who have never even met! The challenge is never greater than when there is a big turnover of people on that team. The showrunner has to ensure that, though writers come and go, the voice has to remain consistent.

You may think that the showrunner is God in this universe; well, that's because it's true. So, if the showrunner is God, at this point you need to have your Transmedia bible to inform the key personnel, be they producers, directors or writers, who are working on the story. The bible will outline exactly what is in this universe and how everything, from character to plotline, has to behave within it.

You also need everyone to know where you want the story to go, what your three or five-year plan is and how you want to develop the story. The bible should provide the key personnel with the means of answering all their questions about writing for your show. Accordingly, only when you have worked out your vision and plan for the show can the story writing begin in earnest.

Old Story + New Media = New World

I mentioned the term 'unique story'; however, when we wrote Sofia's Diary I asked myself what made it different from other diaries about teenage girls? The concept of a teenage girl's diary in itself is not different; before Sofia's Diary there were 100,000 teenage girl diaries and there will be another 100,000 after it, so it's hardly unique. The important point was that, in 2003, we were seeing a revolution in the way teenagers were using the internet and mobile phones. At this time, mobile phones and the internet were becoming social and entertainment tools. What we did was to use these new internet, social media and mobile phone applications to bring characters really close to the audience.

When I say 'close', I mean these new technologies allowed our characters to become friends with the viewer. The internet allowed our characters to become far more intimate with the audience than they ever would have with a character from television or a book. When a person watches television or reads a book they form a connection with a character that lasts just for the duration of the reading or viewing experience. When the programme ends or you finish the book the person is completely disconnected from the character.

The internet enabled us to bring these characters into the daily or hourly lives of the viewer in exactly the same way that they would interact with their friends. The internet also enabled us to further enhance this real-time experience by running the interactions in sync with the audience's life. To do this, we created characters that were living at the same time as the audience. Then, in the story we could coax engagement from our audience using specific 'push tools'. The audience were being texted, coaxed and confided in on their internet web sites, just as one friend would to another. Sofia was telling them there was something happening in her life; but not only that, she needed the viewers to talk to her because she needed their help. By using these new tools, we moved away from passive storytelling, where the audience sits back and observes the characters in action. Instead, the characters were always living, always updating and, most importantly, always engaging with and challenging the audience to get involved.

What is critical to the success of this involvement is that it has imitated exactly what the audience expect when they go on the internet. Typically, internet users have a lot of distractions, a lot of other activities running side by side. We realised that it is vital to keep your audience communicating back with you, because if you don't engage with them they'll quickly get busy with the billion other distractions on the internet. Beating the distractions is just one element of this interaction; the other, is keeping the tone of your engagement consistent with the tone of normal communications between friends on social media, blogs, etc. We knew our show had to be more than a video episode - there can often be a video element, but that wasn't enough to really connect with our audience. The irony was, in order to make our product successful and exceptional, we had to mimic all the normal, everyday things friends do. We realised that, if this was to be successful, it had to be about more than just telling a story; it had to be about creating an experience.

Real characters, just like real life

What was different about Sofia was that, as there is so much drama in the life of a typical teenage girl, all of Sofia's dramas and crises seemed normal and credible no matter how frequently they occurred. Along with all the drama, she also had to be like the girl next door, someone that you could conceivably be friends with. It was vital that it felt real without, of course, pretending to actually be real.

However, we found that, although we had disclaimers telling viewers that this was a fictional story, the fans wanted to suspend disbelief. The only way I can explain this is that the viewer found it altogether more rewarding to act as if Sofia was a real person. The only comparable analogy I can think of is, oddly enough, from the world of professional wrestling. Fans of professional wrestling know that it is choreographed entertainment; however, by suspending disbelief somewhat, they get a far more rewarding experience than if they were watching the show through a critical eye. The same is true of Sofia's fans - they knew she wasn't actually real but, by interacting with her as if she were real, they got a far more rewarding experience from the show.

We found as we developed Sofia's Diary that by mixing reality with fiction we could underscore the character's connection with the viewer's life. I discovered if the character lives in a parallel world with the viewer, certain events should be in sync between the story world and the real world. For instance, if there is a public holiday in the real world, the viewer will expect to see some reference to it in the character's world.

You can take this a step further, as we did on Flatmates, when we removed the normal walls between reality and the story. In this show, we had one character who worked as a barmaid in a trendy Lisbon bar. Accordingly, once a month we set up a shoot where the character went and worked in the real bar in town and we filmed the episode there.

Fans could then apply online for tickets and would also be invited to take photos or shoot clips on their phones, which they would then post on their own social media profiles. These activities provided a very literal connection between the show and the personal world of the viewer. As the photos went viral, the distinction between the lives of the viewers and the characters gained a life of its own.

Two-way communication but not too much control

As we unfolded our story, we were conscious that we would closely mimic how people actually used and communicated on the internet. For example, if Sofia had a dilemma - for example, she was torn between having to comfort a friend or go out with her boyfriend - she would ask the audience for advice. The way she did this was also important, as she asked them as any friend would ask another.

Accordingly, Sofia used MSN, text and email to communicate with her audience and the audience would then reply back with advice. As this two-way communication evolved, we would always make Sofia mail her audience and ask for help. Then, the audience would give their opinion. But it was then that we were presented with a problem - what do we do with their advice?

When we started the show, there was no video element so therefore it was blog-based, SMS-based, and email-based; we could write in the morning and publish in the afternoon. We would then wait for results overnight and incorporate the viewer's desired plotline the next day. We realised after a while, however, that if you give your audience power over the story they will get rid of your antagonist, solve all the major problems and erase all the drama. If the audience connects with your hero they will do everything to protect their hero and solve all their problems. We found if you allow the audience to decide the basics of your story you would be in trouble; after a month, your hero will be wealthy, have the most romantic love-life in the world, best friends in the world, best parents, go on the best holidays and nothing bad will ever, ever happen to them.

Fortunately, we realised this early on and so created what in television terms is called the 'A plot'. The 'A plot', or main story plot, has to be controlled solely by the writers. Accordingly, the audience could not touch, interact with or in any way interfere with the 'A plot'.

What they could alter was the 'B plot', which contained all the minor episodic dilemmas that were contained in Sofia's life. The audience, for instance, would be told of a choice; they could then decide if Sofia should study or go out with her new boyfriend, etc.

We also realised early on that the audience weren't so much interested in the importance of the decision, but rather were more fascinated with the consequence of that decision. For instance, if Sofia didn't study, but went to the movies with her boyfriend, the audience would wonder if she was going to fail her exam the following day. This A plot/B plot divide had the great benefit of protecting the main storyline while, at the same time, rewarding the audience for their engagement with the characters.

Choose your media... carefully

When you are writing a story for Transmedia, the first thing you do is write the entire story with all the elements, twists, character reactions etc.

The next stage can be a revelation for some writers. For instance, when we were producing Sofia's Diary in the UK, we initially hired television screenwriters who had no experience of Transmedia. So, after they had written the storyline they were a little shocked when we took their scripts and literally tore them apart, divvying up the different story elements between the different media available.

Where particular material is used, essentially content is best suited to a particular medium. For example, a conversation that perhaps included a bit of comedy would go to radio. An action scene would go to television. A monologue containing some private thoughts would go to a blog. For you to do this, you have to make sure you choose the media best suited towards the content of your show.

The question 'what media should I chose?' is closely linked to 'how often should I use it?' Ideally, there should be a sense that the content is always updating, that the story and your characters' lives are constantly moving in parallel with the viewer's life. In Sofia's Diary, we wrote one episode per weekday, but there was always this sense created through blogs and social media sites that the characters were always there to update the audience with their perspective. Through all the different tools available, you can create an ongoing conversation and engagement with the viewer.

Be interactive

Television is a passive communication process. Most of the time you sit back and watch and, when it's over, you forget about it and the viewer's connection with the characters is gone. A show on the internet, however, needn't be the end of the connection; instead, it is the start of the next part of the story. It works to re-engage the audience because, when the viewer goes to follow the story on the internet, they may get an opportunity to give their opinion or advice on a character's latest dilemma. A crucial consequence of this method is that once they give their advice on the internet the viewer is more likely to watch the broadcast to see how the dilemma is resolved.

A good example of this type of rolling engagement was Flatmates, which was a show where we had one guy and two girls living together who were constantly at loggerheads with each other. Accordingly, the audience was encouraged to champion an individual and urged to vote to punish one of the rival Flatmates. The punishments included having to cook for a week, clean the bathroom etc. We found that a viewer who is engaged with the character and becomes involved enough to vote has become part of the process themselves. This level of involvement means they will come back the following week to see how their input has played out. Once they are back, you have a new opportunity to involve them in the process all over again.

Tailoring content

It is important to remember that storytelling on demand means that you have to tailor your content precisely to the different people who are consuming the show on different media. Remember, you can't have the same content playing out on every media simply because the audience expect to get specific types of content on each specific media.

When people first started developing video for mobile phones, they made the mistake of believing that success was guaranteed if they provided the television content that viewers accessed every night at home. In fact, this approach was a total failure because the experience people were looking for when accessing information on their phone was completely different to the experience they wanted when sitting at home on their sofa. If someone was going to use their phone to access content it was more likely they wanted short-form material instead of a one-hour documentary. Accordingly, now the audience expect that each medium has its own language and that content is tailored to conform to that medium's particular language and style.

In all the shows that I've worked on, I have had to keep reminding myself that I can't expect all the audience to follow all the media; they may, in fact, be following the story on just one or two separate media. Each medium, however, should be a rewarding and pleasant experience in itself and any viewer should know what is broadly happening in the story simply by following just one or two media.

How this works out in practical writing terms means that you need to study the user to see how they consume information on that medium. For instance, when you listen to the radio you might be driving your car, walking or sitting on the train. This level of distraction means that, for the radio, you need short, sharp informative bursts. Likewise, since you tend to be doing little else when watching television, it is typically delivered in half-hour blocks. When you move to the distraction-filled internet, your typical available window of opportunity shrinks to a relatively miniscule 3-5 minutes and so the writing needs to be clear, simple and concise.

Small screen intimacy

One of the things that surprised us when we started writing for the small screen was how physically close the screen was to the viewer. An argument, for instance, would take place much closer physically to the viewer than if they watched it on television. We found that the viewers found this proximity to confrontation a far more violent experience than the same scene played on television.

On the positive side, this intimacy makes it more likely that you will view the characters as your friend. One of the things we learned early on is that, if characters are to appear at close proximity to the viewer, they have to be appealing. If the character works well and engages the viewer in the first place, then the writer has the opportunity to create a real bond between viewer and character. Personalised interaction intensifies this experience as the viewer gets SMS messages and emails directly from characters.

This type of intimate contact means that, through the characters, you are likely to develop a deep engagement with the viewer. Once you develop that relationship you will find your viewers returning maybe several times over the course of the week to read a character's blog, view photos on their Facebook pages, vote in a poll, etc. You can interact with the viewer all week long. This is one of the biggest advantages of Transmedia storytelling.

A simple way to further develop this bond between character and viewer is to flesh out the character's back-story on their blog and Facebook pages. When we were producing Flatmates, we asked all the actors to bring photos of themselves when they were at school, first communion photos, home videos, etc. We then put all this information on their profile pages and literally gave the characters a real past, thus enhancing their simulated reality. Using photos essentially mitigated any disruption that would occur to the viewer's experience when accessing a social media page.

Cast size

Another lesson we learned along the way was that stories with just two or three main characters work better than ensemble pieces. If you think about it, an online cast the size of The Sopranos, all with their own storylines, would be very difficult to continually track on a 24/7 basis. Transmedia stories draw the viewer so close to the events that the viewer tends to focus and connect with a small core cast. This connection was, by and large, solely with the main character in Sofia's Diary or with the three main characters in Flatmates.

You can, of course, have a large cast of characters in a Transmedia show; what you have to remember, however, is that the most effective way to create a Transmedia experience is to choose a small number of characters from the cast to concentrate on. This is because the level of engagement that is required of the audience to follow their characters is of such an intense nature that the average audience member would not be able to sustain this intense engagement across a large ensemble cast. I would advise accordingly that you choose just one or a small number of main characters for the audience to be 'friends' with.

It makes sense when you consider the way a character will text and write in the blog about their issues and dilemmas. It takes a level of commitment for an audience member to interact with this type of communication. It simply wouldn't be feasible for them to interact in this manner with several different characters.

Small screen language

Directorially you should also be aware of the small size of the screen and compressed video files. Remember, video on internet is still highly compressed and colours are not as vivid as television, so you need to avoid dark scenes and scenes with a lot of contrast. We had to fire one director on Sofia's Diary the day before the shoot because her vision for the show was all silhouettes, long shots and characters against white lights. In a feature film, it would be amazing but on the internet no one would be able to see it. The visual language of the internet is much more compressed, simplified and straightforward.

Being creative

From a creative writing perspective, by using Transmedia you can develop many more perspectives on the lives of your characters. Because you have so many more platforms available, as a writer you can say more and the viewer can keep finding out more about an incident or perspective. It is vital, of course, that each individual media should have some content exclusive to itself. The golden rule in the Transmedia writing process is that the content should be complementary and definitely never contradict itself.

Here is a simple example of different Transmedia content telling the story of three guys who decide to go surfing:

• In the morning on the radio show we'll hear the phone conversation between character A and characters B and C making the decision to go surfing. Typically, this will be a fast piece of entertaining banter between the characters.

• Airing later in the day, the television show won't have the phone call, but will use all the great visuals available showing the guys surfing and enjoying their day at the beach. You may have a reference to the invite from character A but not the entire conversation.

• That evening, one or two of the characters might write a blog telling about their own personal perspectives on their great day at the beach. Characters B and C might thank A for the idea and then go on to write about their own experience and perspective on the day.

• The same evening or next day, some of the characters may post photos of the day on their Facebook pages.

This is a good demonstration of the different ways you can tell the same story using different outputs. Importantly, you don't have to include all the steps in every media. Each output works as a standalone story. The advantage for those who follow everything is that they will be rewarded with a multilayered perspective on the story and a very rich experience. For those following just one medium (say, the radio), they can follow the story without having to read all the other outputs (like the blogs, for example).

It's a simple story with each element adapted to a particular media, thus allowing the writer to flesh out the character's life. I remember when I first did radio, I had to learn quickly that, if you don't get to the point immediately, you've lost your audience. It has very useful applications because, although we try to create characters that do more than just deliver silly gags, the radio provides you with a good opportunity to inject comedy into the story; it keeps the drama intact while, at the same time, makes the scene a fun experience. The writer can visually realise their characters in the video element and through the Facebook photos. At the same time, blogs provide writers with a lot of space to develop a character's inner voice. The combination of the elements should give a really deep understanding of who these characters are.

Again, a key point here is the simplicity of each element of the story. This simplicity is vital, as you have to be careful not to exclude the casual viewer by turning the story into a puzzle. Remember, if it's overly complicated you will just lose people. My advice would be to be aware of the need to keep the story simple and don't be afraid to repeat certain pieces of information.

While the viewer tunes into your show, all those other internet distractions are always just right there pulling at their sleeve, trying to grab their attention. Therefore, a little repetition or redundancy in content is, I think, pretty essential on the internet. Don't try this on television or the radio, however, or else the viewer will just think you're wasting their time.

Transmedia: tricks and pitfalls

Something worthwhile to note is that, by using different story elements on different media, there are endless opportunities for the writer to move the story forward. One successful technique that writers for cop and detective shows on television have been using for years is to encourage the audience to problem-solve before the characters have themselves discovered the answer to whatever puzzle is at hand. In most television detective shows, the audience is given sight of key clues that allow them to come to a conclusion that is usually about the identity of the person who committed a crime. In this way, the audience watching the programme is encouraged to engage with the programme to do some problem-solving and draw their own conclusion before the answer is finally revealed by the characters.

This sort of teasing can be played out in a myriad of ways using Transmedia. I recall we used a similar technique in one episode of Sofia's Diary when a character posted on her blog a Youtube video of Sofia's boyfriend with another girl in a club.

The blog post happened hours before the broadcast of the daily episode, but of course Sofia doesn't know about it. The audience knows about the incident in advance and can predict that Sofia will find the video in the episode that issue will be raised. The video clip is like a ticking time bomb under the entire episode, teasing the audience who will want to watch the consequences. We got a huge reaction to this by providing the audience with knowledge beyond what the characters know about an issue. I think it is worth bearing in mind as a general technique to drop clues and hints to the audience, to give them a wider perspective and use that to engage them with the show.

Cliff-hangers and teasers also provide opportunities to remind you of your hero's mission and keep you involved. The cliff-hanger device may be deployed in a number of ways by a writer seeking to engage the audience for the next episode of the show. The device can be used simply to get the audience to return for the next episode to see how a problem gets resolved. Alternatively, it may allow you to reiterate the conflict between the hero and the antagonist who is forever trying to frustrate the hero's mission. In Transmedia, you can of course use your various platforms to heighten tension and even to give the audience clues as to how the problem may eventually be sorted.

There are, of course, certain tools that can be useful if you want to engage specific audiences in a more interactive manner. For instance, for some audiences we found that gaming was an invaluable tool for drawing the audience in to a show. Final Punishment was a show we did in Brazil that encouraged the audience to engage with the show to save the lives of individual characters.

Set in a prison in Brazil, an episode would typically challenge the audience to save the life of a prisoner who was otherwise going to be killed (in advertisements and messages before the broadcast, we would feature a character using the catchphrase 'Tonight I will be killed, it's up to you to save me'). The audience would then choose from various options how they thought the problem could be resolved. In a way, the show was like a puzzle or interactive game for the audience to solve. Accordingly, because it had these elements, gaming tools were available to the audience to connect with the programme. Obviously, this sort of gaming wouldn't be appropriate for every audience; in this case, however, because the show had a largely young male fan base, these gaming elements were crucial to the show's success in engaging with that base.

We learned early on that you have to fight every day for your audience because it's never guaranteed that they will consume your story. The internet is not like the television world, where a bad show yields a 10 per cent drop in audience share. In television, if you have a bad show on a good time slot, you may suffer a drop in viewers but, in all likelihood, retain thousands or millions of viewers.

In the internet jungle, no audience is guaranteed as you need to fight for, attract, engage, pull, draw you audience in through a dense tangle of distractions. The good news is you can create reasons for them to come to you. Just creating compelling stories isn't enough, though. You have to do more to fight through all the demands on your audience's attention. You have to create something that the audience likes and will make time for; crucially, you have to constantly remind your audience that they like to watch it. The internet offers you the tools to really engage the audience.

Because you want the audience to feel a familiar, intimate connection with the characters, it's important at the outset to keep the situations interesting, which involves drama; at the same time, you have to keep the story real so the audience can identify with it. Most of the stories have to be normal and keep to identifiable situations. Since Transmedia offers you a chance to capture a global audience, you will want to ensure your story is relevant to viewers anywhere in the world. Be aware, though, a story told through the English language doesn't mean it will be an international story if it lacks a familiar emotional narrative. However, a story of three students sharing an apartment is an international story because people recognise this as being a commonplace scenario; almost everyone goes to college, has similar experiences and thus can relate to it.

Keeping it real and keeping it simple gives you the advantage of being able to explain what your show is about in your online logline. It's a brutal reality of the internet but, if you are not able to explain it on one logline, you will not grab the audience and they will never come to you. This line is a gateway to your show and has to be simple and focused on what your story or hero is about.

From the writer's perspective, creating this logline has the benefit of focusing you on what the overarching theme of your show is about. Your story will always have to resonate with that theme and whatever mission the hero is on. For instance, 'Sofia is a teenage girl who asks for your help to survive high school' - in that statement, we have a clear understanding of what Sofia's Diary is about. It's clear, relevant and readily understandable to the audience. Incidentally, because radio writers and copy writers at advertising agencies have to write in such a simple rhythmic style, I've found they have a great advantage when it comes to writing the direct and concise language needed for the internet.

Chapter VI
Produce Content for Multiple Platforms

- What to produce
- Cast and Crew
- Technical production
- Time management
- Union issues

Produce Content for Multiple Platforms

I now want to discuss some of the defining features of Transmedia and how we can focus on the production of the necessary content. There are, of course, a wide variety of different media to choose from to distribute your content. For instance, can they have games or not? Can you use blogs or not? Can you use radio or not? However, simply using one of these elements doesn't necessarily mean that you are producing a Transmedia project.

One of the core Transmedia elements is the online video element. I call it a core element, and one that we will focus on here, because it helps distinguish Transmedia production from other, more traditional, media. Also, I want to have a look at a few Transmedia production tricks that, I hope, will help you develop your story in a cost-effective way.

What to produce

A web series can often be the ideal starting point for the deployment of Transmedia. However, if you are to choose this route, beware of some common misconceptions about what is involved with a webseries. For example, in the past a webseries may have simply involved a character speaking directly to the audience on a web cam. Now, while this had the benefit of being a cheap and easy way to tell a story, after only a short while the device became so overused that people became bored with the format. That is not to say that this type of device isn't useful. Indeed, it is, because it can create a deeper level of intimacy as the character is speaking directly to you, the viewer. I will say, however, that if your series is 'just a webcam' then you're probably in trouble.

Of course, if you're doing a web series you may aim in the future to have a television series or a feature film out of your Transmedia story-world. Despite these very normal great expectations, your funding at this point will be quite low. I mention aspiration and funding here because it's important to realise early on that you need to produce on a low budget; you also need to be realistic about what you can produce. On this point, you should bear in mind that webseries production budgets are usually lower than television or indie film budgets.

Many webseries producers make the common mistake of trying to make a bad copy of their favourite television shows. Remember, your favourite programmes probably have the budget to do as many car crashes or CGI explosions as they want, but you don't. Secondly, audiences are very clued-up and are used to the level of sophistication that accompanies a Hollywood summer blockbuster with a multi-million dollar budget. Sadly for you, this means you can't produce a series whose story demands that level of sophistication (and budget). Really, the only exception to this advice is if you are producing something that is a recognisable parody of an existing mainstream production. If you get it right and your rough special effects result is a funny product, then your audience will be more likely to forgive your cheesy production techniques.

It is also important to remember that your web series at this stage is not just a platform to tell your story. Crucially, it is also the calling card for your entire enterprise; it is what establishes your presence in the market and is the visual representation of your story-world. It also will be the first thing your potential investors, partners, sponsors and broadcasters will learn about your story.

To be blunt, this is the public face of you and your product; if you screw it up here, this is what people will think you will deliver. The point is that your lower budget shouldn't be an excuse for lower quality content; you have to find a way to produce something that is of high quality within your financial confines. This obviously presents a dilemma for most productions: how can you deliver a high quality product with a limited budget?

My answer to this dilemma has always been that you are better off delivering something small that demonstrates you have the talent to create a high quality product. Remember, you don't have to be definitive here about your story. You don't have to lay out the storyline or even introduce all your characters. You can focus on one small element or character that can act as a sort of representative sample of the story-world that you are aiming to create.

For example, if you're doing a sci-fi project you have to obviously remain cognisant of the fact that audiences are typically used to the $200 million dollar production model. Obviously, this scale of production isn't available to you but that doesn't mean that you can't develop some specific aspect of your story. You could, perhaps, focus on your hero's early years, which may require less, if any, special effects and could perhaps be easier to produce. Audiences understand the prequel concept and this could provide you with a sample of what you want to achieve through one character realisation.

However you eventually achieve this, the important thing to remember is that you don't have to try to tell your entire story here. What you are aiming for is a quality representative sample of your work that will tease prospective partners and investors with the potential of your product.

You might also be glad to know that the idea to go low on budget and high on value isn't confined to small production companies. Large media corporations have realised that, aside from budget savings, there can be an intrinsic benefit to launching a small aspect of the story on a web series.

For example, in 2009 when Warner Brothers were re-launching Terminator they produced a web-series using Machinima (Machinima uses computer game engines to real time to produce computer animation in real time). Warner Brothers used the

Terminator web-series as a means to develop the back story of just one character. They didn't try to replicate the full movie; instead, they just fleshed out this one character and thereby engaged the audience. This is a good example of producers choosing a very narrowly defined part of the story (in this case, the Terminator universe), exploring this facet of the narrative on a web-series and then using it as the entry point into the broader story universe.

Cast and Crew

When it comes to crewing, whenever possible I would advise you to use very professional people. I say this, even if your best friend is an amateur actor straight from drama school and is offering to act the part for free. This may be the easiest path to take, and normally people take the path of least resistance. However, to my mind, the path of least resistance in production terms will lead you straight to a minefield.

This really is a quality issue and I think if you are prepared to work a little harder, and are prepared to get a few rejections along the way, you will get quality screen talent. It will be time well spent if you seek out professional talent and spend the time negotiating perhaps a couple of days' work from them. Also, in my experience, I wouldn't necessarily be discouraged by actors' television fee scales as, in many cases, you will find professional actors are willing to work for a lower fee for web-based productions. This is, by and large, down to the fact that actors and professional crew may want experience on new media and are willing to take on the work for a lower fee, thus yielding you a win-win scenario where you get quality screen talent that doesn't break your budget.

If you have a television or feature film background, you will be aware of the way that many people in the industry define production value as a combination of good lighting, design, clothes, sets, props - these elements are what normally yield quality production value. Again, budget constraints mean that you can't just write a cheque to buy this kind of quality. If you wish to achieve high quality, you are going to have to spend more time in preparation. As a simple rule of thumb, if you don't have the necessary cash to put into your production, the more time and preparation you are going to have to invest.

Obviously, these are not abstract notions as they relate to each and every stage of the production process. For instance, you probably won't be able to hire someone to check out possible locations and you will most likely not have the budget to build expensive sets. Instead, you will need to go and physically seek out the best possible location, take care of any required permissions or permits and negotiate a location fee. You will have to follow up with a technical visit with your director of photography, and watch the flow of light during the day to determine the best time to shoot. You may realise that the direct sun at noon is too strong and will have adjust your schedule accordingly. You may find that there is a lot of noise from cars, machines, planes, air conditioning -

things that can ruin a production. These are things that you can deal with ahead of time by thinking not just about what the place will look like on camera, but also whether it will work as a film location on the day.

What you don't want to do is waste any part of a filming day to issues that could have been resolved before your cast and crew arrive; otherwise, you will find yourself paying a lot of people to wait around while an otherwise avoidable problem gets resolved. Again, preparation is key. Of course, things will happen that you won't have planned for, but if you do everything you can to minimise them you will generally achieve the high production values you are aiming for.

One thing that many people don't consider at all is the number of extras that will be required. Unless you are one of those people who have fifty of their closest friends ready, willing and able to hang around your filming location for a few days, I would recommend that you avoid scenes that demand a lot of extras.

Incidentally, this advice applies as much to television companies as it does to webseries productions. I recall this point being hammered home one night a few years ago when I was watching an episode of an obscure UK television series. The episode started off with characters talking about a party they were going to attend that night. However, when the party was shown it was clearly shot at midday because they obviously couldn't afford to light the location in a night-time scenario. To make matters worse, they obviously hadn't budgeted for extras either, because there were only about six people at the party.

The worst aspect of this example of on-screen chaos was that they were all avoidable problems. What the producers in this instance forgot was the quite obvious fact that, if you're not able to make a scene work, you shouldn't film yourself trying and failing. If something doesn't look convincing on screen, the audience (and anyone else) won't make excuses for you - they will simply turn off. The good news for you is that if you prepare properly you needn't make any of these kinds of basic errors.

However, it doesn't mean that you absolutely have to limit yourself to only one or two characters. The point is, you just need to be careful not to overwrite. This means being realistic about your abilities so that your net result is a small scene that works instead of a bigger one that disappoints.

Technical production

As far as the technical production side of things is concerned, the good news for film-makers and creators is that high-quality production tools have become a lot more inexpensive in recent years. I just want to note two examples of this technological change that has brought high-quality content within the reach of most independent producers:

Cameras

With the advent of digital cameras, it is quite possible to buy a camera for a thousand euros that can shoot content of high enough quality for broadcast on television. Also, because digital cameras are more sensitive to light, they require far less 'assistance' in that you don't need as many projectors; in addition, your crew can be smaller as you won't need a full set-up of lights. These advances have allowed us in the past to employ a few tricks to get better film quality on a lower budget.

For example, in 2009 we were filming 'Final Punishment' in different prisons around Brazil. The type of location meant that we would require a cinematic look, as anything else would really jar with the look and feel of the place. The problem would normally have been solved by shooting on a Red-camera, which would have been prohibitively expensive for us to undertake at the time. However, by using the new Canon 5D camera, we were able to achieve a film look that we wouldn't otherwise have been able to do. These digital photographic cameras (DSLR) are becoming increasingly popular; for instance, the season six finale of 'House' was shot using this camera. The advantage of using these new photographic cameras is that the sensor is so big it allows you achieve much better look with less lights, effectively emulating in some respects 35mm film quality. This is achieved despite the fact that you are using a camera that costs just a few thousand euros. That being said, these cameras have their limitations compared with the top of the range models, but if you work around these constraints you can achieve something beyond anything you could have before.

Another point worth noting is the fact that steady cams, which typically could cost thirty thousand euros to buy in the past, are now available for as little as two thousand euros. Also, apart from their increased financial attractiveness, they are now much reduced in terms of weight load, which makes them far easier to handle.

In terms of ancillary camera equipment such as cranes, dollys and so on, by using these on a lower budget you can grab shots that, when they are timed correctly, can enable you to really impress an audience with your production values.

I would say, however, if you are going to hire this type of equipment, once you have access to it you should make the most use of it by filming as many generic shots as possible. You can then, of course, use these shots again and again throughout the duration of the series. Thus, by acquiring a crane or a steady cam for one day, with planning you can concentrate on using them to the maximum effect and plan where they can be used to provide material for promos and forthcoming episodes. The point is, you won't be able to afford them every day, so carefully plan how you are going to use this type of equipment on set.

Edit station

As computers have become so much more powerful it is possible to edit your content on a thousand euro laptop using post-production editing software. This, of course, fits into a broader pattern where software costs are falling across the board. An Avid system used to cost more than a BMW but now can be bought for less than a ten-year-old Fiat.

If you opt for Final Cut Pro-suite to edit and grade, the package now costs less than one thousand euros. Final Cut Pro-suite includes Color app which, a few years ago, used to be a tool that would typically cost more than twenty thousand euros. Now, however, you get it for free with your editing software, which allows you to do the necessary grading or colour correction for the series.

Quality isn't compromised here either, as you can quite possibly finish and grade for any television or feature film using this technology. A word of warning has to be inserted here though - just because these inexpensive, production tools are available to you, it does not guarantee that you will automatically achieve the best quality.

It may seem obvious, but you have to learn how to use these devices, or hire someone who already does, if you want to get the most out of them. What I would advise, if your budget allows, is to use professional people who have the skill-set that will give you the quality product you require. The benefit of this cost reduction and the availability of laptop editing shouldn't be seen purely as an opportunity for some DIY post-production. What it does allow you to do is hire an editor (without having to pay two hundred euros per hour to a post-production house to edit your work), because the big equipment cost that used to exist has been greatly reduced.

Visual Effects
Even on 'ordinary' drama you may want to consider using the new tools available for visual effects, such as After Effects. For example, when we did a Sofia's Diary scene in which a character was killed in a hit and run accident, it presented a challenge over and above our normal everyday content. We decided we didn't want to shoot the scene in the usual tired and formulaic way, wherein the guy sees the headlights of an oncoming car and the action is then cut to the next scene showing the dead body on the road.

However, we didn't have the budget for a special effects team to produce the accident scene. Instead, our editor went to a site called Video Co-pilot, which was a website that provided tutorials for After Effects. The editor studied a tutorial on car-crash video effects and then was able to recreate that special effect in the edit suite. By doing this, we managed to save the cost of hiring a visual effects team by providing some extra editing time. The result was actually very convincing and provided a quality not normally seen on a web-based series. Again, it underlined for me the importance of creative preparation if you're constrained by your budget. Also, if you need to allow your team to get new tools, you need to provide them with the time and space to learn how to use them.

Buy or rent equipment?

There is no clear answer to this, as it really depends on a number of variables such as your budget, the number of productions you have in train, etc. With Sofia's Diary, for example, we used to buy equipment, shoot with it for a season and then sell it second-hand at the end. It worked out quite well for us as the depreciation was, in nearly all cases, lower than the three-month rental cost. In one particular instance we were lucky to hire a Director of Photography who could supply some of his own equipment. This worked out quite well for us and I would advise you, where possible, to hire someone who can supply their own equipment. It may be cheaper to hire someone who already has this equipment and who knows how to use it, than to pursue either the rent or buy options.

If you are using the latest technology on your production, be sure to team up with the people who are using that technology. Good crews will normally be up to speed with latest technological developments, but it is still important that you match man/woman to the machine you're using so that nobody is learning on the job. You can aide this process along yourself. For instance, when we bought our digital cameras for the Final Punishment shoot, we gave them to our Director of Photography two months ahead of schedule so she could get used to how they handled. It goes without saying if you want to use lower budget equipment to get a higher quality result you will need to know how exactly that equipment works. What I mean by this is that, if you want to get the absolute most out of your camera equipment, you should make sure that extensive testing is carried out using the equipment.

If you provide the time, and a little money, for this testing process, not only will you save these resources during the shoot, but you will also get a much better result in terms of quality. The testing will allow you to be realistic and plan your scenes around the limitations of the camera equipment. Also, by matching this type of equipment with a good crew, you will maximise your chances of achieving a really high level of quality.

If you are commercially creative you can sometimes find ways to get your equipment at no financial cost. We managed to do this when we did Sofia's Diary in the UK. We approached Sony Electronics, who were launching a new camera at the time, and we asked them to loan us these new cameras so we could be the first to use them in our production. In return, we agreed that Sony could use Sofia's Diary in their PR campaigns as the first series shot using these cameras. This arrangement had a dual benefit for us as, apart from getting to use the latest equipment free of charge, by using the programme material Sony promoted us throughout their marketing campaign for the cameras.

Time management

So far, I've been implicitly extolling the benefits of good time management throughout this book. However, I want to underline the point that time management is crucial, crucial, crucial when it comes to Transmedia production. I say this because, if you are producing for Transmedia, you are constantly producing different content for different media. You will find the required content list is always expanding, whether it be extra footage associated with the web-series, web blogs or radio promotions. Because your budget will be limited you will want to get the most content out of your cast and avoid, wherever possible, having to hire other voices for, say, blogs or radio shows.

However, with a little planning you can get the most out of the shooting schedule. Anyone who has been on a film set will know that it is normal for actors to wait for hours between setups. Believe me, you will be very aware that you are paying the cast just to hang around waiting in their trailers or in the green room.

The solution is that, if you have your characters there, you are always better off taking full advantage of their presence. In this way, filming days can therefore become fuller production days if you can schedule your characters to record pieces for the radio drama, have a stills photographer present for blogs, publicity and even perhaps have a camera on hand to shoot extra footage for blogs or video games.

By scheduling actors and content in this way, the process will cost less money and will be the best use of the production budget. This point becomes especially pertinent if you are working with higher paid actors. As the one or two days you have them for filming may frequently be the only window you have, you have to get the most out of them when you have them present. I have found over and over again that the hardest part of dealing with top-end talent is to get an opening in their schedules. If you miss something and then have to call and get them to come back, firstly they mightn't be available for a long time and, secondly, it will probably cost you the price of a first class ticket to fly them back to you.

Of course, if you are using filming days as production days for a variety of platforms, it is vital that the Showrunner is present on the set and controlling all the content and not just monitoring what is being filmed for the webisode (for more details on the role of the showrunner, see Chapter V). He or she has to keep an overview on all the content being produced that day so they can maintain consistency across all the platforms.

The showrunner needs to keep this overview and does this by working with the individual producers to identify the specific content needed on each specific platform. Long-term, this involves identifying the content that should be produced over, say, the length of a season on a particular medium. Specifically, this will involve the showrunner working with the various production teams to produce scripts, identify locations, costumes, etc, while always ensuring that consistency across the platforms is maintained.

In a sense, the showrunner has to maintain an overview on everything all the time. They have to be constantly watching and managing output so it stays in sync across all the platforms, identifying what material is needed for websites, blogs and, in terms of content timing, when it'll be needed and when it will have to be produced.

You may also consider another idea to maximise your yield from your actors. One idea that I would recommend is giving your actors some handy-cams to shoot themselves away from the set while in character. This type of unscripted format can be surprisingly useful to give the audience glimpses of their characters. We did this on Sofia's Diary, where all the actors provided footage taken when they were on holidays. It provided us with enough footage for a very successful summer extension to the main series. The quality wasn't fantastic because it was shot on handy-cams, but this was compensated for by the fact that it was very intimate with the added benefit of some novel locations.

We did something in this vein on Flatmates, when we asked the actors to bring their own photos of themselves for us to use on their blogs. We also asked them to shoot footage of themselves while on their mobile phones, and while they were involved in more personal activities like going out clubbing, walking on the beach etc. We could then use this as material on blogs, Facebook sites, etc. In this way, the audience could get an insight into the characters' lives, which had a very authentic ring to it, reinforcing the sense that these characters behaved like real people and had real lives.

Although it's important not to overuse this method, interestingly it was one of the rare occasions when the audience responded positively to lower quality material, which almost gave it a seal of authenticity.

It's important as a producer to remember that this material isn't the basis of a webisode and that it shouldn't be overused, which means you shouldn't populate your website with footage that makes no sense. It's a fine balance, as it makes your characters come more alive, yet you don't want to overuse it so it makes you look like an amateur.

One method we used over the years to get better talent was to work closely with specific talent agencies and develop relationships with them. This takes a bit of time to do, but every year we have a series which then gets exposure not just on the web but on a variety of different media. It didn't take too long for the talent agencies to recognise that our series were an effective place to showcase their new talent.

After a while, we arrived at an arrangement with a talent agency that was to our mutual benefit. The agency agreed that, when they had new talent, they would let them appear for a lower rate in order for them to gain exposure. In addition, following on from this arrangement, they were very co-operative when we were trying to get the top talent to appear on the series.

The opportunity to get top actors to take part, even for a few film days on a low rate, was a great boon to the show. This happened in part because many established actors wanted to gain some webseries experience, but was made possible because we had this mutually rewarding relationship established with their agency.

What is key for an independent producer is not to be afraid to develop this relationship with talent agencies. Take time to consider what the benefits are for them to be part of this production. Focus not just on what you can afford, but also what you hope to do in your marketing plan, emphasising how the series is projected to expand its profile across various platforms, and the resulting benefits this involves for their clients in terms of increasing their profile. For this to work, you have to make the agency feel comfortable enough with you so that they can recommend you to their clients and present the arrangement as a win-win for them.

I will also say that, if you're producing a series that needs a lead actor, you might look beyond the existing lead actors and instead try an actor who is more often playing a supporting role. If you offer them a lead role, despite the reduced rate, you have a good chance of hiring them; you are providing them with a leading role credit on a production, which will be invaluable to them going forward in their career.

Union issues

Wherever possible, you should have professional crews and professional actors. The good news is that, in the in US, UK and Canada, there are now new rules for new media production that allows you to hire professional talent without paying the feature film or television rates. This means that union personnel can be hired on lower budget productions.

Also in the UK, PACT (the Producers association) has established new rules that allow the new media to be seen as a new medium and provides for a new regulatory system within new media for the talent and producers. These types of agreements have made it possible to agree contract rates suitable for web-based budgets in a straightforward manner that benefits both the producer, recognises the requirements of the medium and provides actors with an entrée into web-based production.

Chapter VII
Content Distribution

- Stage 1: Build and online entity
- Stage 2: Growing your brand
- Stage 3: Gaining market visibility

Content Distribution

Early on in the planning and development process, the Transmedia producer has to decide how to maximise the number of people who are consuming their brand. This should involve a plan setting out how you intend to maximise not only your audience, but also the broader awareness of your brand.

This plan is your distribution strategy. The distribution strategy includes planning your marketing strategy and deciding on when and how you will roll out new content across various media. It will be your blueprint to raise your market visibility and guide the continual building of the brand profile.

The distribution strategy has to take account of three, broadly defined, stages of the development of your product:

(i) Developing the product and launching it as an online entity.

(ii) Growing the product, doing deals with other media partners, and then moving into offline media in the form of brand extensions.

(iii) This stage involves the greatest market visibility as you move the product into television, possibly a feature film, and realise the potential for licensing deals.

Of course, this is only a broad development template and can be adapted to suit your particular experience and opportunities. You may, for instance, have been lucky enough to do offline deals early on in the development, or stage one process. Or perhaps you may have a pre-existing brand or television show, and you may wish to adapt that product into a Transmedia product. Wherever you are on the development timeline, I think an understanding of the three-stage linear development model will be helpful as you create your Transmedia product.

We have already seen how you can develop the content of your product across these stages. I now want to look, in more detail, at how we deliver this content to our audience and how, by planning a strategy around this content delivery, you can successfully move through the development stages.

Stage 1: Build and online entity

Stage one of the process involves the initial launch and release of content. At this stage you have your bible, you are beginning to get funding and you are about to release it to the general public. This usually involves publishing on your website, perhaps a digital book, maybe casual games for mobile phones, apps for social media etc. It can include a web series or an animated web series, or (as we saw in Chapter VI) can be launched using Machinima-techniques.

At the end of this process you will have identified your platforms and content. Now, you have to think about a distribution strategy to drive your audience figures.

Partner up

At this crucial time in your product development, you will find that partnerships are key both to driving growth and also to shortening the learning curve. Consider, for example, the television company that perhaps knows nothing about books - if you want to publish a book you will likely want to partner with a publishing company. What the publishing company will do in this instance is hire writers who will then extract a concept for a magazine or book based on your bible.

If you are not a feature film company you might want to license a film company to extract a concept for a movie, again using your bible. There are a multitude of partners each bringing a specific expertise to develop your story. You may, however, feel that you need some partners more than others. You may consider that some areas are completely outside your comfort zone whilst others may involve skills that you can master yourself. Of course, partnership means letting go of some control (and revenue) but it also can often provide some invaluable expertise without which it would be very difficult to develop your story.

With this in mind, it may be useful to briefly consider some of the advantages and disadvantages of partnering with professionals in various media at this early stage of the development process.

(i)Publisher partnerships

If you want to develop a book and you're not familiar with the publishing world, you should give some thought about what route you should take here. If you are not a novel writer, you might consider hiring a writer. Once you provide the writer with the bible and book template, your hired scribe will write your book for you. But once the book is written – what then? How will you get it onto the bookshelves?

Well, you can of course self-publish, and the fact that 'e-books' are becoming more commonplace these days is a reflection of how much easier and faster the whole self-publishing process has become.

Equally though, you should be aware that publishing on your own means you will be making the investment and bearing the costs up front. Secondly, you will have to learn the rules of marketing, promoting and selling in the publishing world. Generally, going down the DIY publishing route means, while it will be more difficult for you to make a success of your book, the great advantage is that if it is successful you will gain a bigger revenue that you won't have to share with a publishing company.

What I would advise is that you should go and meet several different publishers and, even if you collect a lot of negative responses, their feedback will help you shape what is required of your book. So, even if you decide to self-publish, take some time to meet with the professionals because at that stage their advice will be free and you will find at least some of it very beneficial.

Finally, you can go down a more traditional route and partner with the publisher. The advantage of this option is that the publisher will bring to your book all their business know-how and marketing skills. Crucially, they will also validate your idea and let you know if it is compatible with the current market trends. The disadvantage with taking on a partner here is that you have to share the revenue. From my own perspective, I think that they have a wealth of advice and information, without which it would be very difficult to go down the book publishing route.

(ii)Web partnerships

One key element of this distribution strategy is to have a web distribution partner, who will heavily promote your content. It is important again to remember that, just because you launch your story on a website, there is no guarantee that you will get an audience for it. In the first instance, to get an audience you need to make people aware that you exist. You can slowly build your own traffic to your website or, alternatively, you can piggyback on another company's existing traffic. For this to happen, you need to partner up with, say, a newspaper or some other already successful website to drive audience to your content.

Normally, I will tend not to create a lot of different websites for a story but instead partner with one internet portal (e.g. Yahoo, MSN etc). For Sofia's Diary UK we used Bebo which, technically speaking, isn't a portal, but the concept is the same (they can be best likened to an internet channel where your content can be found). The idea is that, if the portal likes you, they will promote you to their audience and potentially promote you to at least some of their millions of visitors.

Alternatively, if you have an independent website and you do all the marketing yourself, it is unlikely that you will be able to match the audience traffic that an established portal can provide you with. The key person here for you to contact and convince is the partnerships manager of one of your portal companies. Following on from this, several deals can be done. They can ask you for money for them to market your story. Alternatively, they may find your content very interesting and pay you for the privilege of having your content on their website. Or you may do some sort of revenue share deal where they will do the promotion, you provide the content and you split the resulting advertising revenues.

You should be aware, however, that if you are in the business of producing content for children and pre-schoolers you will encounter significant barriers unless you choose the correct web partnership model. For starters, young children don't search like adults do. Instead, they will go to a broadcaster's website or a recognised kids' company website. In Ireland, for instance, they will go to the RTÉ, the public broadcaster, website and play the online games provided there. Typically, they will have their favourite sites and will stay there for a long time. Also, because they are constrained with cyber nannies and parental supervision, they are far less likely to move to another site. I am mentioning this because it is important if you are doing kids' programming to get your content such as games, puzzles and activities featured on a broadcaster's portal. Otherwise, the likelihood is that you could be blocked out of your target market.

(iii) Games partnerships

Developing computer games is an area outside the expertise of most people. Accordingly, I would say that the standard route here would be to contact a games company and pay them to develop your casual game.

If your story already has traction with an audience, they could pay you for the licence to develop the game. The best option early on, however, may be to agree a co-venture with the games company where they develop the game under licence and then, by agreement, you can split the revenues.

I recommend the co-venture route when you're starting out. Firstly, at this point you won't have the money to risk in developing a game on your own; secondly, it will bring in a useful revenue stream. Remember, your story can also then be piggybacked on the games companies' own marketing material to their existing audiences. This type of arrangement is extremely useful when it comes to spreading your brand and widening your community.

(iv) Apps

As with games, the development of apps will, in all likelihood, be beyond you unless you are a software company and are able to develop these in-house. It is, however, very straightforward to establish a partnership with a software company to develop these quite inexpensively.

(v) Radio partnerships

The idea of setting up your own radio station obviously isn't an option here.

Therefore, if you are going to have radio content, a partnership with a broadcaster is the only real approach open to you. Remember, when you approach a radio station with a view to partnering with them, you need to bring your story bible and demonstrate that you have a clearly realised concept for the proposed radio show. Without a detailed and clearly realised programme concept you will be unlikely to get very far.

Ideally you should find the radio station that attracts a similar audience to your story's target audience, and then do a deal with that broadcaster. The best-case scenario, when doing a deal with a radio station, is an agreement where they pay you for the licence for your story. Alternatively, you might have to pay the radio station to broadcast your material.

However, I have to confess that I have never agreed either type of deal and always ended up agreeing to give the broadcaster the content for free. The big benefit for us, though, was that we agreed a co-marketing agreement with the radio station that allowed us to expand the public profile of our story.

Controlling your partner

It is vital, as you partner up with other companies, that you maintain an overview of how your product is being represented. It is up to you to keep all the outputs in sync with your bible so there is no disruption or contradiction across any of the media.

Beyond this, you also need to stay appraised of the various marketing efforts that your partner companies are involved in and create synergies where possible. For example, if a feature film of your story is being launched in May of next year, you might also want to delay publication of the book until then so as to maximise the exposure around both products at the same time.

You will appreciate then that, as your partnerships grow, you will want a marketing plan that doesn't just focus on separate media as independent entities. Instead, you will want a plan that takes an overview of what is required across all outputs. This type of co-ordinated approach, when it works, has much more potential to create a buzz around your brand.

One important point regarding content is the question of who maintains editorial control after you have licensed it to a partner. There will be occasions when, for example, the licensed partner may request changes to the underlying story or tone to help their film. At this point you have to be careful and consider the implications across all other media. You may change the bible if you don't think the effect will be detrimental, but you may also have to say 'no' if the effect of a change would be to undermine the consistency of the narrative across the board.

PR campaign

As I have already alluded to, another key element at this early stage is your PR campaign. This will be focused on how you create as much buzz as is possible around your product. This basic tenet of your PR campaign doesn't change as you develop the product. What is essential is that you plan how you intend to generate new media interest in your story as you grow.

Media, of course, is interested in anybody who is already well-known, be they famous actors, writers or directors. So bear this in mind when you are developing your PR campaign. It is always helpful to have someone associated with your product who will generate interest just by their presence, and who will also talk about your content and mention it when they have the attention of the media.

To illustrate this point, consider for a moment how media interest would be generated by a webseries featuring you and your friends. The answer is, of course, not much. I say this because working with a celebrity will increase audience awareness.

I don't mean you have to break the bank and use the most famous actor or celebrity that comes to mind. Fortunately for you there is currently a near insatiable media appetite for any news about celebrity. Consequently, should you hire a B-list celeb or actor for your series, it will create enough of a buzz that the media will cover your story and the celebrity's involvement with it.

In this way, the celebrity will act as a hook; they may only appear in one episode, even just one scene, but their presence will probably be enough to build a PR campaign on. Apart from the media buzz that the celebrity factor will bring, it also has the added benefit of providing your content with a tag that can draw in more audience on the internet. You will find that, when someone searches for your featured celebrity, your content will appear on the search results, again increasing your profile.

Image

Another issue to remember is the importance of image and visual presentation. It might be a cliché, but you really don't get a second chance to make a first impression; therefore, you need a professionally produced website that positively underscores your product's image. You have got to pay attention to the quality of your graphics and technical quality of your webisodes. Generally, the presentation of your material has got to reinforce the fact that you are a professional producer and, of course, at the same time highlight your brand.

New is news

In the recent past, as new media were being rolled out, it was quite possible to be the first to do something and garner a little publicity on the back of that breakthrough. In 2003, had you produced a webseries, you could quite easily have been the first to do so in your particular country. This fact alone could have got you media traction.

Nowadays, as digital content has become quite commonplace, it's a little more difficult to market yourself as a novel production. However, there are always new ways of presenting things, new artistry and new technical methods to employ. These innovations can form the basis of a claim for media attention. It doesn't have to be earth-shattering news either; you could be using a new social media site or employing some innovative technology. For example, you could claim to be the first to use augmented reality technology in your webseries, which could be a useful angle by which to get traction in the media. A word of warning here - if you are making a claim on innovation, you have to be careful that you can substantiate your claim and make sure that someone hasn't done it before.

Shout about your success

The reason why you should spend time on your media and publicity campaigns at this point is to avoid a really big pitfall. Suppose, at the end of stage one of your development, you have managed to be very successful on the web, have gained a large audience and are getting good feedback about your product. The big danger for you at this stage is, if your content doesn't appear in the offline media, it is possible that you won't get a partner to take you into the next development stage.

It is vitally important that your online success appears in the newspapers, the mainstream media and, of course, industry publications, because you need your potential partners to know about you and your success. Don't lose sight of the fact that while you are successfully building your target audience of, say, teenage girls, potential partners - be they broadcasters, publishers or whatever - may have no idea that you even exist. It may seem kind of obvious, but they won't go into business with you if they haven't heard about you and your success. That's why it is important for you to make sure they know about you, who you are and your online success. It's essentially about creating as wide a community for your story as possible, beyond your target audience, to include your target partners as well.

This wider public profile has, of course, the added benefit of strengthening your hand when you do go to negotiate with partners. In these deals, evidence of broad public awareness of your brand, together with an established audience, is half the battle when it comes to successfully negotiating a favourable deal.

Of course, if you already have an established brand - for example, a television show - you are at an advantage because you have an audience and established broad community awareness. Again, this makes it more likely that people will be willing to do a deal with you. I will say, however, that regardless of how well-known you are, in partner negotiations make use of the fact that your brand has wider community awareness, as well as a quantifiable audience, to press your case for a deal that is favourable to you.

Syndication versus Exclusivity

Dealing with partners, especially on the web, raises the question of whether you should go for exclusive deals or opt for the syndication model. Syndication is the typical model in the United States and has the advantage of your content being available on dozens of websites. This, of course, gives you a wider audience and potentially greater site traffic. The disadvantage is that, if your content is everywhere, none of the portals have a vested interest in promoting you.

Alternatively, I have found greater advantages in exclusivity deals. This is simply because, if your story is exclusive to one particular portal, they have a vested interest in promoting the content. The exclusive deal also allows you to very specifically direct an audience from another platform, very simply and directly, to your web presence.

For instance, on Sofia's Diary, at the end of a radio drama we would tell our audience to follow us on Bebo. In this way, everything we were promoting could be easily followed up on www.Bebo.com/sofiasdiary which was a very simple radio message to communicate. If we had gone for the more dispersed syndication model, it would have been difficult to direct people to our multitude of web presences.

Size matters

Mobile phone applications are obviously important to your success in reaching an audience on this medium. So when it comes to devising a distribution strategy for mobile phones, choosing the right app partner is obviously one of your most significant decisions.

With this, it's important to know a few things about the company that you intend to partner with, such as how many people use it, what its competitors are and so on. This can involve a lot of research and making judgement calls on whether the biggest company is necessarily the best for you. Consider for a moment iPhone apps, which are available in a highly populated store. In this scenario, your iPhone app will be just one amongst the other 200,000. There are, for instance, similar stores such as Blackberry, which are smaller, but consequently you are more likely to stand out should your brand be featured in them.

Instinctively you may think that partnering with the most popular platform is the surest avenue towards increasing your own brand profile. However, I found through my own experience that this is not always the case. When we were making Final Punishment in Brazil, we used two different mobile phone technologies. Firstly, Java was available, which had the advantage of being compatible with more handsets (90 per cent). We also, however, decided to create content for BREW, which was only available on a small number (10 per cent) of handsets.

Because Java comprised 90 per cent of the market, most of the production companies and publishing houses were going to Java. What we realised, however, was that because there were fewer companies producing for them, we had much less competition from other apps in the smaller BREW app store. Consequently, we were frankly amazed to discover that we were getting way more clients from BREW than we were from Java.

I realised after this episode that sometimes a bigger partner may not necessarily be ideal because the competition within it can, in fact, overwhelm your brand. Also, you may find that sometimes the smaller partner may give you more chances and be amenable to striking better partnership terms than the larger app provider. Again, this involves a judgement call as, ultimately, the decision to opt for a smaller provider means that you may be opting out of a bigger potential audience. Therefore, I would advise that you work out the benefits of each provider and see what is already available on each platform. You may discover that the small provider, with the less diverse store, will give you better results.

Co-marketing
In the last chapter, I mentioned co-marketing technology deals whereby your partner may use you as a case study and promote you in their own advertising. In the example, I mentioned that Sony allowed us to use a new camera for free and they then used our material in their own PR campaign for the camera.

Be aware that this co-marketing idea can be applied to a wide range of your partners. For instance, if you are working with particular talent agencies, they may use their PR team to do some co-marketing agreement that involves their talent and your Transmedia series.

I would also advise you to keep your sponsors in mind. They may help you promote your content in their internal advertising material. For us, a successful example of the different layers co-marketing can involve was when Sofia's Diary was sponsored by MOVIFLOR (a furniture company) in Portugal. We had agreed to furnish Sofia's bedroom by using furniture entirely from this company. They, in turn, then re-created the Sofia's Diary bedroom in all their stores, and featured it on some of their promotional literature. For instance, Sofia's room was also featured in two million store catalogues that were posted to homes all around Portugal. We also went with cast members to showrooms at weekends to do book-signings and 'meet Sofia' events, which became very popular with fans.

This type of activity also gave us valuable contact with the audience and helped increase the profile of the brand. The co-marketing deal involved a really positive and rewarding relationship with the sponsor, which saw not just us getting the sponsorship money, but also yielded mutual benefits; for example, we promoted the sponsor a little extra and the sponsor also promoted our brand in their internal advertising.

Remember, the sponsors are not just there to give you money, but can also provide you with a lot of additional exposure and some of their own marketing might. For instance, with Sofia's Diary UK, one of our sponsors was a national clothing chain. They agreed to use stand-ups of our talent, wearing their clothing throughout their stores. It is, therefore, important that you view sponsorship deals as not just opportunities for finance, but also very valuable opportunities for national promotion.

The end of the beginning

It will take time and energy to get to the end of the first development stage, where you will have maximised your potential audience and community. At this point, you should have lots of downloads of comic books, thousands buying or downloading your content (usually free of charge), and thousands using your app or web game. Don't forget, this audience of active viewers and participants are your currency to move on to the next stage of development, where you monetise your content and get the financial reward for your labour. We've also seen here that you will want to generate offline buzz, television coverage, magazine coverage and have a growing number of people talking about you so that more will access you.

As your product appears to grow, your future partners will hear about you and be more enthused about coming on board. I've found that it takes approximately 3-6 months to get this level of development and get the market traction that will yield a sufficient level of exposure. The exception to this timeline was Sofia's Diary in the UK because it was an already proven format, and also we had a huge partner in the form of Bebo.

These favourable factors meant that, early on, we got a big community online, with our online audience for the first webisode reaching five million in the first weekend. In that first weekend, we jumped to month six of our development schedule, transferring immediately to television. This, I caution, is an exception, but it gives an idea of how you should be prepared to adapt your development plans to respond to greater or lesser audience demand than you had initially anticipated.

Stage 2: Growing your brand

As you move into stage two of your product development, you are no longer struggling to exist or be seen to exist. Instead, now that you have proven your brand can attract audiences, you are in a position to approach offline entities for partnership deals. These partnership deals will provide you with revenue and/or increased market visibility.

A word of caution regarding the timescale of these development phases - as regards stage two development, be aware it normally doesn't happen all at once. For instance, when we started Sofia's Diary in Portugal, we managed to get a magazine column from the start. However, the book publishing deal took place six months later and it took a full year before we partnered with a radio station to get the drama broadcast nationwide.

Offline media challenges

These offline extensions can typically include newspaper and magazine columns that your characters will write or a radio drama or a book publishing deal. These partnerships are principally aimed at getting a wider audience for your content than you can online. In an ideal world, you may be able to do stage one and two at the same time, where you grow your online and offline content simultaneously from the very beginning. In fact, as we saw with Sofia's Diary in the UK, this may be possible if you are an established brand.

Normally, you will find that you cannot branch into the offline world because it's very difficult for a traditional offline business to be able to partner with you if you don't possess a proven track record. The problem is that, unless you have built up your exposure and have become widely known, you are unlikely to get past the offline gatekeepers to their audiences.

When you do build an audience and manage to do deals with the offline entities, you will find huge scope to increase your exposure. This exposure has a number of benefits. Firstly, you will find that your audience quickly grows as the daily or weekly offline outings widen your potential community. Secondly, this move into offline also has the added benefit of bolstering your credibility as a producer. It is still the case that, if your content is appearing, say, on radio and in magazines, it becomes both more credible and more respected in the marketplace. I have found again and again that when my content has been endorsed by traditional offline gatekeepers, business brands that people regard highly, it has redoubled the respect for my brand elsewhere.

A note on book deals. The book deal has a singular potential to increase both your audience and your market credibility. I say this because, if your publisher works with you, your content will be featured prominently in the windows and on the shelves of the bookstores. Additionally, if it becomes a best-seller, this in turn makes you respectable and proves you can sell a product - a fact that will not be lost on other commercial partners later.

This point about book deals is really reflective of the widely perceived superior value of offline as opposed to online success. Remember, if you have two million views on the internet it doesn't prove you have brand. However, if you sell products, based on your internet success, it proves in a clearly recognised and quantifiable way that you are finding your audience and that they are willing to buy books and listen to your radio show.

This fact partly has its roots in the early failures associated with the online business enterprises. For instance, when MySpace started, most of the record labels started signing according to which band was the most popular on MySpace. This faith in online success was discredited, however, when most of these signings failed to sell albums in significant numbers.

By and large, therefore you will find that traditional gatekeepers remain sceptical of your product's ability to translate online into offline success. So, as important as it is to develop your product through stage one, stage two is really about showing that you have been able to transfer your audience to offline media. Only by actually showing that you can cross the online/offline barrier can you deconstruct that scepticism surrounding internet-born brands.

This breakthrough is key to the entire objective of the stage two development process. By the end of this stage, you will have increased your brand and community. You will have achieved this by attracting people, who didn't already know about your brand, to you. However, by distributing your content through radio, newspapers, and comics, many of these newcomers will also have begun to engage with your online series. Once you can quantify this process, you will also break through the industry scepticism that online entities are unable to create traditional media success. Then, because Transmedia production never stops, when you achieve this level of success you are ready to move to stage three.

Stage 3: Gaining market visibility

If you define stage two as the development period where you extend your brand into offline media, then stage three is where you develop more traditional or old-form media, extending into feature films, live shows and finally licensing.

New media and old television

Once you have a successful magazine, newspaper or radio column, a sucessful web presence, or sold thousands of ebooks, apps or games, you are in a position to go to a commissioning editor at a television broadcaster and propose developing your brand as a television show. There are huge potential benefits for you in moving into television, as the medium widens your community to new demographics that don't often interact.

Approaching a commissioning editor, and knowing who your show is aimed at, gives you a distinct advantage as broadcasters are always trying to find established audiences. The fact that you are able to provide the broadcaster with a quantifiable, pre-established audience will greatly strengthen your hand. The second thing in your favour here is that you will be able to pitch the brand using some of the visual material you are already producing. For instance, webisodes and comic books are very useful if you want to show what you intend to produce for television.

Incidentally, I would advise that, if you don't have experience in television production, the broadcaster may be reluctant to work with you because you lack a track record. Television is a medium of trust and relationships built up over time. Broadcasters work with companies they have worked with before who they trust. This trust is established over time as producers successfully deliver quality material to the broadcaster.

Therefore, before approaching the broadcaster, it might be wise to partner with someone who already has a good track record and who the broadcaster trusts. Also, if you intend to develop a television series, you may want to bring some writers on board. I say this because creating a half-hour drama is very different from creating a webisode, more particularly because broadcasters will normally focus on the writer as the creative architect of a television drama. This being the case, you should really have someone on board as a writer that the broadcaster can feel comfortable with and trust to do the job.

Once you do a deal with the broadcaster, the television series will allow you to expand your community, not just from the exposure the broadcast receives. The broadcaster will spend a lot of money promoting your show and that will also have a huge impact on your brand. Additionally, if you're also producing books and games, etc, their sales will benefit enormously as your brand becomes better known and moves from its niche to the mainstream. We will focus on the entire product licensing arena in greater detail in Chapter X.

Film

The feature film is distributed on a global basis and accordingly has huge marketing campaigns and media coverage way beyond anything that television can match. Despite the constant challenges and competition faced by the film industry, they still provide by far the biggest stage if you want to turn your story into a global brand. The film community of your brand will be one of the last and most significant communities that you can create. Once you do this, and your product also has a web and television presence, a feature film will make it a truly global brand.

There is another phenomenon that we are seeing a lot of lately, that seems to me a bit like putting the cart before the horse. I'm referring to the fact that some Transmedia projects, early on in their existence, will skip television and produce a film with an ultra-low budget and very little marketing in the hope that they will get an international distribution deal. These projects are usually aimed at a niche market and don't have the big marketing associated with film. The result is that, even though they exist as a film, they have none of the advantages you would associate with, for instance, a Hollywood blockbuster. The project may sometimes have some good content and you may launch it at, say, a film festival, in which case you may get some limited domestic success.

However, I don't think you can count on this to promote your brand unless you get very, very lucky and achieve significant crossover success (I can't overstate how rare this type of success is. Personally, I would liken it to your chances of winning the lottery). By launching with a feature film, you may be mistaking where the real advantage lies in the whole feature film business. The real advantage of the feature film, to you in terms of brand creation, is its huge distribution potential and in the marketing of the movie.

Stage shows, Plays and Live Events

Another area that is becoming more popular is the live show, which these days is associated with almost all the brands aimed at the children's media market. These live shows bring the characters to life with stage shows, puppets etc. Its primary advantage lies in the fact that the live show is a huge revenue generator. Also, apart from the potential financial gain, the show will be promoted and the PR and advertising campaign will add to your brand recognition.

Much like the television business, if you don't have any previous experience you would be wise to partner with someone who knows the industry. You bring the brand, the bible and, of course, the proven popularity. You will need your partner to bring the necessary expertise on how to adapt your content to a live show. Of course, this format doesn't just apply to the children's entertainment industry. If your content is aimed more at adults then you can perhaps stage a comedy show or a rock concert that can help generate extra revenue and gain a wider exposure. It's worth considering the fate of the music industry for a moment and, more precisely, consider the fact that, as sales of downloads and CDs fall, they are sustained by live shows and concerts. Accordingly, I feel it would be a mistake to overlook the fact that live shows are growing because more and more people prefer to attend an event than buy content online.

Therefore, even at the early stages of development, it's worthwhile determining whether it makes sense to stage a live event. Even if you just have an online community, have a look at the geographical spread of that community. You may then realise that a significant portion of your audience are accessing your content online from a certain region or city. The option is then open to you to go there and produce a show in that region that will generate revenues; it will also be a way to get to know your community and extend exposure. Depending on the scale of the event, it might even make sense to have a small play that can travel and generate revenue and media exposure. It will also allow you to further develop your product and closely connect the audience with your story.

This connection is worth considering, as I believe it is a fairly unique benefit of the live show wherein you get a real, close and personal interaction with the audience. Indeed, it is worth considering through all the different stages of development rather than simply at the end as a mass marketing brand. In effect, you can even use it as a focus group for you to get feedback from your audience. However, if you intend to do a larger-scale show, you will likely need to wait until you are a well-established brand and are able to employ the necessary budget and capitalise on a large, pre-established audience.

Managed growth

One key consideration to bear in mind when developing your brand is how you will manage this expansion and the sheer volume of work this expansion may entail. We spoke earlier about the importance of the showrunner in maintaining consistency in the content. The producer, however, will have to leave this type of detailed content management to others as the brand develops. In fact, as the brand grows, the Transmedia producer morphs more into the brand manager, who has to co-ordinate the distribution of the brand and maintain the integrity of the entertainment brand.

It is important to realise that, as soon as you move into the later stages of development, you will be dealing with a lot of other people, from stage show producers, radio and television broadcasters, co-production partners, publishers, licensing companies, etc. As we have noted, as soon as the product grows, you will find yourself becoming less a producer and creator and more a brand manager.

This is important because, in the end, all the partners are working towards their own particular aim; the broadcaster will be focused on making the most successful television show, while the publisher will be focused solely on the biggest book launch etc. They will be immersed in their own activity and won't be too minded about the other content producers. Therefore, you will inevitably find that it will be completely up to you to co-ordinate all this activity so that the greater objective of increasing the overall brand awareness is achieved.

Specifically, this will involve you getting the books launched at the same time as the television show is on the air. Similarly, you may want the live events to run between television seasons so that you can extend audience involvement between series. As I mentioned elsewhere, you will want magazine content to be in sync with radio shows, etc. The list goes on and on. What you want to avoid is a scenario where a book is launched without any on-air promotion. Again, it's up to you to see that this doesn't happen. What this requires is a very broad marketing plan that brings order and co-ordination to the activities of the many disparate groups producing your content. Remember, it's up to you to get everyone's launches, schedules and activities to match up, as only you have the overview.

Chapter VIII
Social Media

Social media

In the last few years, a small communications revolution has taken place as the social media phenomenon has transformed how we use the internet. You see this specifically with sites such as Facebook, Twitter and Youtube, where content is derived from a close and constant interaction with the audience.

The internet has changed so much in the past few years that it is worth bearing in mind how much more content there is now than there was, say, fifteen years ago. Back in the mid-1990s, when there wasn't as much content on the web, sites like Yahoo were able to index the information and provide it rather like a phone directory would. By 2002, it was no longer practical to view indices of material and therefore this method was overtaken by results based on specific searches provided by search engines such as Google. In the last decade, however, there has been yet another paradigm shift as recommended material is increasingly preferred to the random search result.

Back in 2003, when we were starting out with Sofia's Diary, none of these social media tools that are so prevalent now were available to us then. We therefore needed to create the communication tools that you can now find so easily on various social media. At that time, the only similar outlets for this sort of content were blogs. Accordingly, we used blogs for our characters to tell their story. They also allowed the audience to participate by leaving comments and feedback on the blog site. Crucially, this enabled us to create a community of followers of Sofia where they could respond to the content.

At this point, however, we figured that it would be worthwhile to further develop this idea of frequent interaction and bring it to another level. We looked at methods that allowed the character to be permanently in touch with the audience by leaving messages throughout the day, much the same way that a Twitter account would do now. We used this device both to tell the story and also to promote events.

As I say, at that time Twitter wasn't available so we had to achieve the same function using a mobile SMS subscription service. This service allowed the fans to subscribe so they would get daily alerts from Sofia. It proved an invaluable tool in heightening this intimate sense of contact with Sofia. It achieved this intimacy through the alerts by letting the audience know what she was doing through the day, teasing them with what was coming up in the next episode, asking them for advice about a dilemma she may have and, of course, reminding them to follow the story on her blog. The great benefit for us as producers was that the service, with all the audience comments and advice to Sofia, provided valuable feedback from the community we were building.

All these tools were created from scratch. Nowadays, of course, you don't need a mobile subscription service, as Twitter allows for a very slick ongoing connection between your characters and the audience. Using Twitter enables you to publish this type of content and for your community to get updates throughout day.

In the early days, we also established an external forum to allow the audience to post comments and share their stories. This is something that Facebook now allows you to do really well. Facebook also allows you to create your blog, hold discussions, post photographs and post videos. These are very valuable tools that you need to tell a story. In fact, Facebook provides you with all the technical tools that enable the type of up close and personal user participation that you will require.

One of the other benefits of social media is, of course, the reduced costs involved in Transmedia production. Because of these sites, if you want to use online video you don't need to invest in players, servers and all the other tools that were necessary for video content. Instead, you can quite easily use Youtube or Facebook facilities to release your video content and broadcast to your community.

Again, all this vast technological apparatus wasn't available to us when we started in 2003. However, thanks to the huge advances in IT and also the investment that these social media companies have made, extremely useful tools are now available to you to tell your story. Best of all, they already have a prebuilt audience. At the time of writing this book, Facebook has an astonishing 600,000 million registered users.

All of this brings us to a very important point beyond the technological advances and reduced production costs involved with the social media revolution. One of the most important aspects for us to understand about the entire social media phenomenon is the fact that these companies have become analogous to big broadcasting entities, and are now part and parcel of the daily routine of a vast number of people. Hundreds of millions of people now use social media many times on a daily basis and are an established part of popular, mainstream culture. These services, therefore, not only provide you with the services and tools to promote your content and thereby cultivate a community, but also provide you with access to an enormous potential audience.

Popular Services

Since we've been mentioning various social media, I just want to look in a bit more detail at four of the more popular social media phenomena.

1. Blogs
I mention blogs here at the outset as they were the first locations on the internet that created easily accessible forums for ordinary people to publish their ideas, photos and their creations on the internet, and for communities to interact

with this content. In a way, you could describe the blog as the internet's first democratic means of allowing ordinary people to communicate with the world.

Blogs aren't, of course, just an object of historical curiosity; indeed, they still provide you with a practical way for a character to engage in personal storytelling. For Transmedia, they still provide one of the best ways for your characters to express their inner voice and to express themselves. They are also a way to promote discussion and two-way interaction in a very personal environment.

2. Facebook

Facebook allows you to create a fan page and, as I mentioned, provides you with a number of extremely useful services. For instance, you can create a blog, post photos, post videos and a range of other content that will help you start to create a community. This 'community creating' potential of Facebook shouldn't be underestimated, as the site works by allowing people to become fans of different content and material. As anyone who has used the site will know, these fans then get notified when you upload any content to your Facebook page.

It also has a very open API (application programming interface) that allows you to integrate with the core applications behind Facebook. What this means is that it allows you to develop interactive apps and games that can be accessed on your page. By allowing for these extended services, Facebook thereby creates more opportunities for a more interactive experience for your audience.

For example, when we were making Final Punishment, we created a Facebook app that we developed as a viral tool. The app worked in such a way that, whenever you became fan of Final Punishment on Facebook, a news article featuring your name would be generated. The news article said that you were being investigated by police because you were playing the Final Punishment game and the police had launched an investigation into anyone playing this game. This notice, of course, then gets posted on your wall, and all your friends get the fairly eye-catching update saying that you are being investigated by the police. Many of them in turn would check out the content and, in the process, sign up to our Facebook page. Once the new fans had signed up, the whole process began again and their friends in turn were notified that they were being investigated by the police.

This was a good example of when a small, simple app could engage not just the audience but also draw in their friends (and later, hopefully, friends of the friends). This is one of the great benefits of social media, because it works in such a way that your audience can promote your content to their friends and in the process make them part of your audience.

Another point to note about Facebook is the fact that it is fast becoming one of the more media-aware social media sites. You can see this in the way that it is now doing deals with broadcasters around the world, who are themselves extending their services beyond the social media range. These broadcasters are now using tools that allow them to broaden their focus away from the exclusively social media experience, reflecting the fact that producers and content creators want to tap into the hundreds of millions of people that access the service every day.

Specifically, this development is reflected in the way you can now have advertisements on Facebook; for example, if you are starting your own show and wish to create a community, you will want to put the word out there that you have a new show and promote it. To do this, you can now use Facebook advertisements that can be organised in such a way that they are displayed in specific geographical regions, to specific demographics, specific genders and so on. This bespoke advertising allows you to target your particular audience, to show them your advertisement and thereby attract them to your Facebook page where they can access your content.

I just want to reiterate a point we touched on earlier regarding the viral aspect of a Facebook presence. Because of the social nature of Facebook, when you create a fan-base it tends to snowball as the friends of fans themselves become fans, followed by their friends also becoming fans and so on. You will see that when this viral effect takes hold, and communication about your presence becomes more widespread, your community will mushroom.

One significant issue of concern that I would have when working with Facebook surrounds the question of advertising and promotion. Facebook, for instance, will not promote your content unless you have enough money to spend on Facebook ads. Also, you will have noticed that they don't have a home page where they could promote your product or carry a suggestion that people use your content. This restricted opportunity for promotion is not the case with a lot of other media that you could find yourself in partnership with. For instance, if you were to do a deal with a magazine or newspaper website, you would typically get a commitment from them to promote your content. This sort of promotion, especially at the beginning of your development, will then likely give you a bounce by driving traffic to your website. Facebook, on the other hand, will not provide this sort of partnership arrangement to promote content.

So, if you're starting out and solely depending on Facebook to provide your content, it will be very difficult to get the word out about your presence unless you pay for the Facebook advertisements. You will have to appreciate that, because there are so many other entities, communities and applications on Facebook, it will be very difficult for you to get noticed if you don't have another marketing partner that can drive your audience outside of Facebook.

Bearing all this in mind, I would advise a two-step strategy that initially would see you do a deal to put some of your content in a newspaper or magazine website, or an internet portal, or perhaps produce a radio show - all are ideal ways to promote your on-line presence.

By using this strategy, you can use your partner's pre-established audience to generate traffic to your content. Then, in addition to this deal, you can then use the interactive tools provided by Facebook to help you create a community that can interact and participate with your content.

3. Twitter

Over the past few years, Twitter has developed to become a high profile and important social media service that allows you to post small messages or 'microblogs' to people who subscribe to receive your updates. As I mentioned previously, when we started Sofia's Diary we needed a facility that would keep audiences aware of what she was doing. We had to do this using a mobile phone SMS subscription service; however, Twitter will now allow you to do this far more easily and cheaply.

When it comes to deciding what to use it for, I would say Twitter would be important for you generally if you want to keep your audience updated, especially if you want to create a community where the audience needs to receive daily updates.

As far as future innovation in this area is concerned, Twitter is now developing tools that help users get the most out of technology, such as localisation and also the ability to post photos, videos, etc. This video-posting service is a significant breakthrough for Twitter, where messages were, up until now, limited to text-only messages. However, like Facebook, as it is now working closely with media companies, it is introducing new tools to allow media producers and marketeers get more and more from their Twitter account.

Also, just like Facebook, Twitter is also now promoting new forms of advertising to their significant audience. For you in the early stages you now have the option to employ this very focused advertising technology to target your audience. This process allows the audience in the first place to know about your content, engage with the content, and start a new community of people who follow your story, initially through their Twitter accounts.

Despite its relative youth as a medium, there have in fact already been some notable examples of entities that started out as Twitter-based phenomenon, who built their community on the site, before then making the leap into mainstream media. For example, in 2010, CBS in the United States commissioned two television series that were initially launched as Twitter account. In fact, more broadcasting networks are looking at Twitter as both a tool to engage their audience and also to turn successful

Twitter accounts with big audience bases into mainstream entertainment products. A notable example of this includes the recent hit television series starring William Shatner called '$#*! My Dad Says', which started out as a successful Twitter account.

4. Youtube

The other key social service that you will likely want to use is Youtube, especially if you want to distribute video content to your audience. Youtube is the biggest video-based social network. We are all now so familiar with Youtube that it is easy to forget what a radical departure it represents, providing a search engine for video content as opposed to 'traditional' text-based searches. This search method ties in with the way younger audiences access content, as they increasingly abandon text for visual searches.

Therefore, I would advise you to look firstly at the tools that Youtube provides you with to broadcast to your audience, and also to consider how you can benefit from the large potential audience it provides you with for your video content broadcasts. For instance, Youtube not only allows you to put up videos but, crucially, also has the tools to enable the broader Youtube audience to become subscribers to your content, which means that they will get an update whenever you post new content on Youtube.

Apart from this, they also provide all users with the tools to comment and vote on content, thus providing useful interactions between the Youtube audience and your content.

In terms of quality, Youtube also has full HD video capacity, providing you with a platform for high quality video on the web. I should also note that Youtube has recently introduced tools to enable the broadcast of long-form content such as TV episodes or feature films, and also stereoscopic 3D material.

Youtube also allows the user to create hyperlinks, and links embedded inside videos, that can lead you to other sites (e.g. your Facebook site). It even allows you to create images that are clickable objects within videos that can link you to another site, or perhaps a shop where that object may be purchased. You can also experiment interactive storytelling which, after a video finishes, allows the user to click on a choice of follow-on options. It is, therefore, not just a straightforward platform for you to broadcast videos, but also a really creative platform that allows you to introduce a range of interactive options around your videos.

Also, I just want to note that Youtube provides a partnership programme that provides you with an increased opportunity for them to divert traffic to your content. Essentially, it is rather aspirational as it differs from a portal in that, instead of a firm commitment, Youtube will only commit to the notion of diverting traffic to your content. It is not a guarantee, but given the volume of traffic on the site it is definitely worth considering.

Apart from the creative options, it provides you with a number of important marketing tools such as its partnership mode, which allows you to analyse your video community, customise your video page and, most importantly, monetise videos. The monetising option comes into play when you sign up as a partner and allow Youtube to put ads on your videos. Youtube, through a revenue share agreement, will then pay you for that advertising. The last point would make me inclined to advise you that, even if your main partner is not Youtube, you may want them to release some of your content as you may want to access that audience and gain some vital revenue by monetising your content.

5. Other Social Media Services

There are, of course, other social media tools out there as this is a very dynamic market and things can change rapidly. That caveat given, however, at the moment we can say Facebook, Twitter and Youtube are the biggest sites with each dominating their respective arenas, where Facebook is the predominant social network, Twitter the major microblogging site and Youtube the principal video-sharing and viewing network.

There are other sites that provide services to more specialised communities, for example Linkdin is focused on the business niche, as well as other specialised sites like Digg and Foursquare.

Also, regionally there can be rivals to the big sites which you may want to pay attention to. For instance, Orkut, in Brazil; at the end of 2010 it was more popular than Facebook. However, depending on where your priorities are, you have to decide whether your content will be broadly available through syndication or exclusively concentrated on just a few websites where you can focus your efforts on developing a specific community.

In the end, the biggest advantage social media has to offer is the way its sharing and recommendation has become so powerful. Your audiences pick your content and then go on to share it with their friends and family. Hopefully, the friends and family will endorse it and they, in turn, will become the next wave of people to distribute your material.

One social network is better than two

Specifically, when it comes to social networks, you will encounter a problem if you decide to spread your content across many sites. The problem is that, if you opt for more than one site, your community will be fragmented as they won't be united on a single platform, all sharing the same experience. In fact, from my own knowledge of this area, I wouldn't advise you to split your content on different platforms as it makes it far more difficult to create the notion of a single community.

For example, when we were making Final Punishment in Brazil we encountered a situation where Facebook had a 40 per cent market share and Orkut had a 60 per cent share. So we decided to have a presence on both sites. What this meant practically was that we had to develop everything twice which, obviously, is more time consuming and more expensive. Nearly as significantly, it split our community as they weren't communicating together on a single site and comments that were posted on one site, were automatically lost to the other community.

Essentially, because we had to split our presence across two sites, we had divided our audience into two smaller communities with a consequent loss in the quality of the show experience for the viewer. Fragmentation, I later concluded, was not the best approach because, by splitting the community, we deprived the audience of the full overview of both the story and all of the audience interaction.

What we learned is that when you want to create a community you want all of them to have the same experience. You don't want your content dispersed because, whenever your audience is asked to move from one media to another, the simple fact is that you will lose some of them.

Also, the last thing you want is a puzzle of content that doesn't allow you to maximise your connection with the fans. The sole platform allows you to maintain the quality of the experience and keeps the audience united with a single, consistently focused message across one social media service. That, by the way, doesn't mean you should always pick Facebook. In actuality, I would say the decision should really depend on who your target group is. For example, if your target group is children aged 8-12, then Facebook isn't for you as you need to be 13 years or over to join. Instead, you need a social media network that is focused on the specific group that you are targeting.

Why people use social media

There is another important issue to note concerning social media. When you are trying to create a community, you should examine why people are using social networking tools. The evidence suggests that they are using these sites to connect with people, even perhaps spy on friends and acquaintances, to tell friends and family what they are doing, to post videos and photos of themselves and their friends. They are, in fact, mostly concerned with the mundane but personal details of people's lives.

Therefore, I would say to you that, whenever you are creating a fictional character with, say, a Facebook site, you need to be really careful and think about what kind of content they should be posting if they are to engage with the audience. For instance, many companies have made the mistake of trying to get audiences to be 'friends' with their retail brands. This approach misses the entre point of why people access social networks.

The point is, people don't go on Facebook to be friends with a car or a can of beans; they go there to connect with their friends. What they do is go to Facebook to see what their friends are doing and connect with people in a specifically personal way. For example, if your character is a 16-year-old girl, you should be aware of what your audience expectations are for, say, a typical teenage girl's Facebook page, before you create a Facebook page for your character. The idea is that you want to create a connection between the audience and a character who you want to portray as realistically as possible. By creating a fan page on Facebook, you can create something that has all the attributes of a profile page. The fact it is labelled a fan page lets people know the page is not actually real, while at the same time allowing you to create a community of people who want to interact with your character in the normal Facebook style.

Therefore, I would advise you to make the experience as organic as possible. For instance, as regards those people who want to use Facebook to sell a product, perhaps you would be better off creating an alter ego to represent that brand, because it's far easier for the consumer to engage with a character on this medium than with an inanimate product.

For the Transmedia producer, however, the important thing to remember is that ultimately people are on social media to share thoughts, ideas, experiences, photos, with friends; therefore, the interactions and content that you put there have to be consistent with this key audience expectation. That is why characters and storytelling are such an important part of your social media content because, if you create compelling characters and storylines, audiences will be willing to suspend their disbelief and follow the show to find out what happens to them (in the same way as they would if they were following a story about their real friends and family).

Leaders of the social media community

In social media circles, the leaders of the community are commonly referred to as 'influencers'. These people may not be the biggest users of the internet. Their defining attribute is that they have a lot of people paying attention to them and their opinions. What is important for you to realise, if you want to harness their influence, you have got to identify them, engage with them and talk to them. They, in fact, can be quite influential and it consequently may make a lot of sense for you to get them 'onside'.

One advantage of the social media revolution is that the release of news and information is not limited to the major news corporations. Instead of there being a limited number of old media experts, you now have a larger group of bloggers. These amateur non-celebrities have developed their 'track record' and, over time, have become as powerful as the professional newspaper columnists.

On Facebook, for instance, you will find non-professionals with thousands of fans because they articulate opinions, review material, upload content, etc. Similarly on Youtube you have some users who don't create any content but instead create playlists out of their searches of Youtube content. People who like their choices can then subscribe to these playlists and actively follow the choices that the playlist writer has made. These creators of playlists and reviews, are the really heavy users of the social media networks.

They are, in fact, powerful leaders and opinion-makers and, if they like your content, will spread it with their recommendation throughout their communities. If some big Facebook user picks one of your videos, then all of his friends will see your video. So, you should therefore be aware that not all users are the same. Most are ordinary users, but there also exists this subset of leaders who have the potential to introduce your website to their own small armies of followers.

There are some useful methods you can employ to find out who these leaders are and therefore actively engage with them. For instance, when we launched Final Punishment we did a lot of work to find out who were the bloggers about thriller stories, who were the bloggers about video games, group managers of communities on Youtube, Yahoo, etc. After we had done this and identified who they were, we decided to approach them ahead of the launch. So, before anyone else saw the material, we invited this group to a private screening presented with a nice invitation with package, goody bag and some promotional material for our show. It was important that they were invited ahead of the launch because, in many instances, their reputation rests on them being the first to know about a phenomenon.

The follow-on from this is that, if they have the information before it becomes widespread within their community, they will be eager to disseminate this advance knowledge. The bonus is that, when they are spreading this information, they might also say good things about you. It really is worthwhile engaging with this; by picking fifty bloggers you might be tapping their collective fifty thousand followers, thus the potential viral effects are enormous. You need to recall that these guys live to find the next big thing and, if you provide them with a hint that you may be this 'next big thing', they will spread the word about you. That is why it's vital for you to do everything you can to prove you are worth both their attention and their endorsement.

Having first identified who these influencers are, it is important that you engage with them on a personal level. For instance, you may invite them to a screening, and if you do it right they can be your first fans and thus use their power to motivate their fans to access your content.

In fact, I found this to be more indicative of the shift in influence from old to new media than anything else. For us, this initial engagement with the online community was far more important than getting the print journalists onside. Because we started out on the web, it was more important for us to initially engage with people within this realm than it was to get an article written about us in a newspaper.

Social Media challenges

A final piece of advice, regarding social media, involves the ongoing evolution of the phenomenon and how it is becoming ever more complex and increasingly more competitive. You can see this where every media product now has a Youtube video, a Facebook account or a Twitter account. Because of this ever-changing social media terrain, with new entities and trends, creating a community has become increasingly more difficult and requires ongoing research to keep abreast of all the changes in the area. If you want more detail regarding social media, I would advise you to read some recommended texts on social media marketing (see Appendix).

If, however, you don't have the time to undertake the kind of research necessary to navigate social media marketing, you can get someone to do it for you. Thankfully, there are now social media agencies that can promote your content inside Facebook and other sites, as this type of marketing has now become an art-form in itself. I would say, in fact, that it has become so complex it requires a professional to navigate its challenges. Therefore, if your focus is on your story, you should consider hiring someone that knows how to do this.

Chapter IX
International Distribution

International Distribution

Up until now we have seen how an idea may be developed, funded, produced and distributed. In doing so, you will have tackled a range of challenges such as bringing different parts of your product to the market and using social media to engage a community and attract an audience. In short, you have achieved a lot and succeeded in most of your aims and objectives that you had for your brand in the territory or country that you first launched it in. What I want to address here is how you can take that success and use it to bring your brand to an international community and monetise it on a global basis.

The world is your oyster?

We live in a world where, if you post a clip on Youtube, nearly everyone in the world can look at it. Still, I would argue that it is somewhat erroneous to think that you can just post material on the internet and, hey presto, you've got a worldwide fan club. The fact is you will face significant barriers when you bring your brand to an international audience, be it a language barrier or simply the limited reach of your marketing effort.

Just a word of explanation on what I mean by the limited reach of your marketing effort. Even if you have 'marketing partners' who are helping you to push your material regionally, and even though you're on Youtube, it is still unlikely that your brand will spread beyond your territory. As a matter of fact, typically only the Americans really can distribute stories with the marketing power sufficient to engage a worldwide audience. They also have the distribution and marketing power that ensures that their products are not just consumed on their own territory but also are spread around the globe. For example, Glee is now one of the biggest shows on Earth; it was made in America, broadcast initially on the Fox network in the US and then almost immediately afterwards by broadcasters around the world.

This is, however, just one facet of Hollywood's huge media power which, quite uniquely, allows them to create content in one territory and make it immediately available around the globe. Another aspect of this can be seen in the way that Hollywood movies are launched on the same date in the major media markets around the world. In the past, a movie appeared in the US and, if it was successful with American audiences, it was sold to the rest of the world. Now, the marketing campaigns and distribution strategies are global from the word go.

Success starts at home

This is, of course, all well and good if you are working within this US media. However, if you are, like me, not a Hollywood insider then you probably don't have the marketing power or international distribution network that you need to gain instant attention on the global media market. In that case, you may want to think about what you need if you are to try and go global.

The first thing that helps when you are going to the international market is a taste of success at home. What I mean is that you can only sell internationally what has already been success in a national market. Even with Glee, before it became a global phenomenon it had first to be successful in the American domestic market.

Trying to originate and produce an idea in an unfamiliar territory is extremely difficult. So it makes sense that you start by originating and producing your brand in your own country. If you then make it succeed at home, you can then try to convince an international partner it will work in their country. It stands to reason that you have a better chance of convincing an international partner that you can make money in their country if you have already managed to do so in your own.

Of course, there are exceptions to this, such as the film Cinema Paradiso, which was a flop in Italy but was bought and distributed internationally by Miramax and became a worldwide success. I say this by way of instancing an exception to the rule. Still, in most cases, you should wait until you are successful at home first before attempting to find success overseas. Remember, we are working in an industry of hits, not failures, so you need a national hit before you go international.

If your goal is to go international, I would advise you, as you start to develop and produce content, to document all your production processes. This means keeping a diary of all the things that happen on your production, the things that work and, just as importantly, the things that fail. Keep note of your marketing campaign and how you developed and implemented it. Note how audiences reacted to different initiatives. Write and record everything about your production and marketing processes, because this will be your biggest asset when it comes to communicating to international partners about how you successfully produced your brand.

Write your cookbook

In effect, your production diary should be the raw material for your production cookbook. Your cookbook will list all the materials, scripts, set designs, tricks of production, outlines for film shoot schedules, how to organise content, marketing strategies, partnership relationships and so on. It will contain all the information on what you need, and what you need to do, to achieve success with your story. Importantly, the instructions and the meanings have to be very clearly expressed so they can be replicated in another territory and produce a broadly similar result. It needs to be a self-explanatory document detailing all your experience and communicating to the international partner exactly what they need to do.

Remember, when you go to sell the concept everyone will want the cookbook. This is nearly as important as the content you are selling. You should bear in mind how difficult it was and how much time and development effort it took you to achieve success. There was much trial and error, but eventually you hit upon a winning formula. The idea here, then, is to eliminate this development process altogether for your potential buyers, who will just want a ready-made hit and the sure-fire steps to making it happen. The bottom line is that your prospective international partners are not just buying your story content, but the knowledge of how they can replicate this on their own territory.

Which is better, format or product?

If you produce something that was a success in your own country and you go through the process of documenting what worked and what didn't work, you are ready to go international. There are now two approaches you should consider:

1. You may want to sell as a finished product. This essentially means that you sell your content as it is to an international partner, who will re-broadcast it in their territory. This fairly straightforward process works best when you are selling a show with high production values, made in an English-speaking market. Because English is a universal language, even if the show is subtitled or dubbed, the industry is already adapted, meaning that you can sell the content and your cookbook to non-English speaking markets. The great benefit of this approach is, of course, that you do not have to reshoot your content. Regional partners that take your content to broadcast regionally will have to invest less money than if they have to license a format and produce a local version.

However, because the show's cultural accents and attitudes will not be local, it will be difficult for audiences to have a close connection with the story. This will be the greatest challenge you'll face. For arguments sake, it would be very difficult to make the first version of Sofia's Diary work in China because it would be quite hard to persuade viewers that this Portuguese Sofia is the girl next door. This is why, on Sofia's Diary, we decided to license the format and have a local Chinese version of the show, adapting scripts and using local actors.

What this boils down to is that an audience will tend to identify with a show set in its own cultural milieu, more than it would with a show produced overseas. A prime example of this phenomenon can be seen in the way the domestic audiences in the UK respond positively to their home-produced X-Factor and American audiences respond to American Idol. The audiences for these shows in their home territories are immense while, when they are broadcast overseas, they acquire nothing like the same level of audience interest.

Because of this, Sofia's Diary had to be produced in every territory it was broadcast in. Obviously, some shows don't depend on this close, intimate level of engagement; but for those that do require the audience and character to connect, it's better that they have the same cultural references.

2. If, like me, you have a low budget and are producing content in a territory with no tradition of exporting audiovisual content, you may alternatively opt to sell the format of the show. This involves selling the idea and the cookbook which, as I've described, outlines the production process. I also found this option to be especially attractive as, when I was producing content in the Portuguese language in Brazil and Portugal, I found it made more sense to sell formats that sold this content directly into other language markets.

However, one of the disadvantages of this approach is that, if you are to sell all these different local versions of your content, it will cost your buyers a lot more money. This is simply because it will cost the local buyers of the show way more to reproduce the content than it would if they were to simply subtitle or dub a pre-existing show.

You also have to consider the fact that we are living in a global market. If local versions of your story are being produced around the world, audiences in one territory will be able to access content in another. You can, of course, try to block people from accessing original content but audiences will always find a way around geo-blocking.

This becomes a bigger issue if there's a mystery or a puzzle used in the original story that you want to repeat in overseas versions. You have to think about what the effect would be if these later audiences can access the answer to a mystery contained in the earlier, original production. For example, consider for a moment the film The Sixth Sense. This film worked because of the big reveal at the end of the movie. If, however, the reveal was commonly known, it would damage the show. Geo-blocking and spoiler alerts are, of course, a help; but where games are involved, you may want to change the passwords or clues that you use in the different versions so that the audience is genuinely challenged. Again, it will require more work, but this way you can actually keep your product as fresh and enjoyable in a foreign territory as it was in the original.

I should note here that you should not, by any means, regard the idea of audiences in one country accessing content in another country as a bad thing in itself. As I mentioned, even though content was geo-blocked, part of the audience will find a way of accessing it. In fact, one of the surprising things we found was that audiences, who were curious about other 'foreign Sofias', found it quite rewarding to look at these other shows about Sofia that were being broadcast in other countries.

In many cases, we received feedback that suggested that viewers found it an interesting cultural experience to see their familiar story and characters played by other actors, speaking in different languages in a different cultural context. Regarding the overall question of whether to release content as a format or a finished product in international markets, you need to balance these various considerations and choose the option that best fits your own content and circumstances.

Alternatively, you can adopt a two-stage approach to your international distribution. This approach was used by the owners of High School Musical where they successfully released the American version of the movie onto the international market. Then, on the back of its worldwide success, they created local versions of the same story in key territories around the world. They used local actors and largely the same plot and storyline, which didn't contradict the American movie. For me, this is the best approach as it has the fastest rollout, helps to create brand awareness and maintains brand unity amongst the different versions.

Going international - your choice?

There are occasions when the decision to go international may actually be decided for you by a financial imperative. This issue will probably arise if you're producing a feature film or high quality television series. You will find that, because these types of content are so expensive to produce, they need to be distributed in several territories in order that the project investors get a return. Consequently, when you are planning your deployment strategy, you need to take this under consideration.

You will understand this need to be careful when you start producing content that overlaps between territories. For instance, if you started producing content in the UK and then produced a movie based on this UK content and then also licensed the format to the Australian market, you would be faced with the problem of keeping all of this content consistent for each audience. The danger is that a movie based on UK content could be confusing to the Australian audience if it is based on events that have yet to occur in the Australian produced story. For instance, if you made adaptations to a British character, they may contradict something in the Australian version of that character, which doesn't make for a pleasant viewing experience and can be quite jarring.

Global contradictions

Once you have settled on the idea of rolling out content in different countries, it is extremely important that you settle on an international distribution strategy as comprehensive as the one you devised for your home market.

I say it's important because, once you partner up with international partners, you will find competing agendas that may work against the interests of your brand. As always, it is up to you to devise a strategy that protects your brand and keeps you in control of the overall marketing strategy. In fact, it is in everyone's interest that you keep this level of co-ordinating control so you can head off the types of disputes and contradictions that would inevitably arise if international production partners were given a completely free rein over their marketing and distribution plans.

When you are thinking about international content you have to consider what elements from the story-world will transfer into different territories and what elements will not. What I mean is, you should do something like a feature film that is intended for international distribution, which can then unite all the audiences. Obviously, an internationally recognisable film is more effective in this regard than something locally produced and culturally specific such as a blog or webisode.

As a case in point, when we started to think about a feature film of Sofia's Diary, we were immediately faced with the question of who, from the many Sofia actresses, would be in the feature film. What we came up with was an idea of a 'Sofias reunion'. This involved actresses from all the different territories playing a part which obviously had the advantage of giving all the different audiences a familiar foothold in the feature film. Of course, this is only one solution for this issue faced by one story, but you need to give consideration to the international contradiction and resolve it in a way that unites rather than divides your network of international audiences.

Who will buy?

It goes without saying that, if you are to sell your product internationally, you will need to know who your buyers are going to be.

Imagine for a moment that you are a television producer, selling a television show. Your buyer in this case would obviously be a broadcaster. Similarly, if you were only selling mobile content you would sell it to mobile phone companies and, if you were selling web content, you would probably approach internet portals. However, for the Transmedia producer who is creating so many different kinds of content for so many different platforms, the key question is who do you sell to?

The answer to this question wasn't at all clear when I first went to sell Sofia's Diary internationally. Initially, I tried to sell the different types of content separately. So I found myself arriving in a country and then launching into an endless series of meetings. This strategy saw me pitching to a television company one hour, a mobile phone company the next, a radio broadcaster after that and maybe an internet portal after that.

In all of these meetings, it was very difficult to explain that I was selling one aspect of the content of a wider story. In fact, when I was trying to sell a television show, I often found that the different media would distract the main buyer. It was quite common for the broadcaster to wonder if they should have their internet people involved in the meeting because I mentioned that the show also included internet content.

I figured that the idea of trying to sell several related things at the same time was just too confusing and distracting for individual buyers. What I realised was that if you want to get buyers you have to play by their rules. In the normal course of events, purchasing and acquisitions managers are used to buying certain defined products. For instance, they buy movies or they buy drama series; in fact, you'll find that most broadcasters have individual buyers for different products.

So, after wasting many months on chasing a lot of different buyers, I can now give you some advice that I hope will save you a lot of time. What you need to do is focus on a few different types of buyers:

(i) Independent production companies

You should approach independent production companies around the world with a view to them buying your format, which grants them the rights to adapt and produce your Transmedia format in their specific territory.

What I like about this sale scenario is that, when we approached companies, we not only offered the scripts and format but also some important commercial relationships with the global brands that sponsored us. For example, in a number of cases production companies could go to their local Gillette media agency and tell them that they had the rights to do a show called Flatmates. The producers could then request that, when this same show was aired in Portugal, it had Gillette sponsorship. In this way, the sponsorship deals weren't exactly ready-made with the format; however, because there was a clear precedent, they were much more straightforward to clinch. This not only made it easier for the production company to get their sponsorship, but it also made our format more attractive in the next territory we approached.

(ii) Broadcasters

The other route you can take is to approach broadcasters and pitch solely the television element to them. Then, when you make the sale you can offer them the opportunity to license your mobile phone content, web content, etc, in that territory. I found this to be the best way to focus the broadcaster on what they usually do; once that key element was concluded, we could then move on to talk about other products. It is important to keep the initial focus on the television element and then introduce the other types of content. I have found, to my cost, that by trying to negotiate with all the content on the table you will only distract the broadcaster and ultimately bog down the negotiations.

(iii) Media agencies

More and more media agencies are creating their own entertainment departments so they can sell this genre of content to their clients. For example, Steve Coogan recently starred in a webseries funded by Foster's beer. This is part of a growing trend as media agencies become more comfortable with web-based content. In this way, they are increasingly looking to distribute content in a multiplatform way with, of course, their brands attached as the main sponsors of the show.

(iv) Internet portals

Internet portals are other possible buyers for finished web-based products. They have seen how increasingly important it is to cater to audiences who are focusing more on video and less on text. Accordingly, these companies are now licensing web video and looking for exclusive deals on content, so they have a competitive advantage in their territories. So, what you are selling to portals will largely include short-form content, webisodes and perhaps games. As the money on offer is very low, however, these deals will mostly be concerned with taking existing content and then dubbing and subtitling it.

(v) Mobile phone operators/aggregators

Normally, these companies are looking for short-form video content and mobile games/applications to license them in packages to mobile phone operators.

(vi) Video on demand services

These services may be Digital TV Box (provided by Cable, Satellite or IPTV operators) based or internet based. They are worth targeting, especially if you have a television series or feature film to sell.

How to sell Transmedia

When we started producing Transmedia content, nobody, including industry professionals, knew what it was; therefore, if we wanted to let people know about what we were doing, not only had we to produce the content, we also had to distribute it ourselves. This was largely down to the fact that basic awareness of Transmedia was quite limited in the media world at the time, so there was nobody you could approach who you could licence to distribute your brand. There were big television and film distribution companies but nobody was doing the same for Transmedia.

So, early on we were going to the markets, such as MIPCOM, MIPTV and NATPE, where we would set up a stand and sell our format rights directly to potential buyers. We had to go to these market events to first explain what we were doing (because there was no understanding of Transmedia out there) and then to sell. It was expensive and time consuming, but still we needed to do this because we had no real alternative way of selling Transmedia internationally.

Nowadays, a few international television companies have Transmedia departments. For example, in the UK you can go to companies like i-Rights or Content Film, both of which have departments that are focused on selling web and Transmedia content.

You can go to one of these and you can license them under agreement to represent you internationally. The advantage of going to one of these companies is you don't have to attend markets, hire a stand (which are quite expensive) and sell your product directly. This allows you to spend your time on what you do best, which is making content. In addition, they have a big catalogue of buyers that they can sell your content to, thus making the process very straightforward compared to what it was.

The disadvantage of hiring a company to sell your product internationally is that you lose the connection with the buyer. For us, when we didn't have a middle man we worked directly with companies around the world, which allowed us to gain a clear understanding of the particular terrain of these markets and their differences, culture or content needs. This kind of close contact with the international partners allowed us to really feel the pulse of that market. So, a word of advice here: it stands to reason that when you're not talking to companies directly, you won't get the same handle on what they really want. Despite even the best efforts of a really good agent, there is no substitute for direct contact.

The other big disadvantage is, of course, that these agencies have many clients. It stands to reason that the amount of close attention your product receives from them depends on how important you are to them. You also should bear in mind that, not only are they selling other companies' content, but they may be also selling their own product, which may take precedence over yours.

The key thing to remember is that ultimately there is no definitive right or wrong approach to international distribution. If I was starting now, I would probably go to an international agent to distribute my content and I would concentrate on producing it. However, for you, I would say you should weigh up all the options and, in the final analysis, decide what will work best for you and your brand.

When you arrive at a situation where you have successfully sold formats into different territories, you will then have to balance a lot of different (international) interests. When you were growing your brand, in all likelihood you developed it in the three-stage process that we discussed previously. This would have seen you build up a number of partners and platforms incrementally. While this happened, you needed to learn how to manage the different competing interests, from the different partners and companies, and make them work harmoniously. You needed to co-ordinate all these diverse groups of people and companies involved to optimise overall growth of the brand, and get the maximum benefit using a cross-media marketing strategy.

As you begin to sell formats of your content in various territories, you will need to specify which media these formats apply to. You may, for instance, sell the format of your web or television series to a local producer. However, your storyworld may also have a book or a film. You will not want a situation where the local producer has the rights over all your content in 'their' territory and have the power to perhaps block the distribution of your film there. Accordingly, you should be able to limit the form that can be localised and limit the format license to each particular media. By limiting formats to specific media, if you then produce a global book it can be available in every territory, as you reserved some rights to certain media to be distributed by yourself globally.

If you thought that sounds complicated, bear in mind that once you go global, not only will you be managing local radio, newspaper, publishing, television and internet content at home, but you will also be faced with the challenge of how to manage content world-wide. In effect, your responsibilities for co-ordinating the various interests in your product are multiplied according to the number of partners you now have in other countries.

There are other challenges regarding global content management that we alluded to before; for instance, if you're thinking about publishing a book or releasing a feature film that will be distributed in different territories. Also, bear in mind that, if you are licensing a company to make, say, a toy based on one of your characters, you will usually license them internationally. So, when it comes to licensing products, it is critical that you know how this key element in monetising your brand ties in with the marketing strategies across the territories that your product is available in.

Global strategy

At this stage in your development, the important thing for you to realise is you can't just have a local plan, or even a collection of local plans. You now need a global strategy. Your global strategy will need to lay out exactly how different elements, especially the internationally distributed elements, interact with one another. For instance, it will state exactly how a book or feature film, that will be available around the world, will integrate with your local content.

At this point of development, you will find that you have 'graduated' from being a content creator to an international marketer. Of course, on top of this the strategy has to be backed up with a will to implement it. I recall, for the American version of Sofia's Diary, the local producers wanted to change the age of the main character and make it for a young adult audience. This, we felt, would involve corrupting the story in the United States, as it would also mean that the product licensing (aimed at teenagers) wouldn't work in the American market. Since our global distribution strategy was aimed primarily at pre-teenagers and teenagers worldwide, it meant we had to insist that Sofia remained consistent with her original age. For me, it was a clear instance of the global distribution strategy maintaining that harmonious interplay between the competing local partners, where each wished to shape the original product to fit their own local concern. If you surrender to the disparate local forces at work, you will lose all the potential synergies that make a global brand cost-effective and profitable.

It's probably wise, therefore, to keep in mind that the best way to achieve the best result is to learn how to work with partners. Essentially, you have to find a way to make them want these global synergies.

The best way to do this is to incentivise them to implement your view, i.e. if your partners have a share in the profits they'll want to help maximise them. Usually, this share would be worked out on a local basis. For instance, if you are publishing a book that will be distributed in several territories, your partner broadcaster would get a share of the royalties from the book sales in its particular territory. It's the old story - money talks - and I have yet to find where a share in royalties has failed to encourage harmony and make local producers pay attention to the global dimension.

That is not to say that it's not difficult to manage (it is), or that you still won't have to compromise (you will). But remember, too, that you can't be too prescriptive; you will always have to let the local content producers adapt your brand to the terrain they are familiar with, or else your show won't be produced.

Local hurdles for your global campaign

Usually, advertising and marketing campaigns are planned on a region by region, territory by territory basis. This obviously increases costs, as the same tasks are replicated in every territory where your content appears. Nonetheless, despite the cost benefits, global campaigns are still something of a rarity outside the big Hollywood system.

This rarity is really down to the myriad of different cultural hurdles that have to be considered that increase with the addition of new territories and regions. Different things have different meanings and significances in various cultures. Consequently, you should aim for a 'one size fits all' marketing campaign. For instance, when we made Sofias Diary in China, we had to increase the age of the character, because her character and behaviour just wouldn't have been convincing had we used the standard European age. These kinds of changes obviously have consequences for devising a global campaign where the characters themselves vary quite significantly.

You need, therefore, to be careful of the cultural challenges that arise that can place blocks to a wider global distribution strategy. You need to know how the story will be consumed in different territories. You need to know how the audience in Asia will react, what the Latin American audience will think, or whether the European audience will like the content. The very last thing you want is a situation where the European audience responds positively to a story but, at the same time, the show fails all over Asia because it violates some cultural law.

This obviously creates challenges for you when trying to navigate this international cultural maze. However, it's a challenge that can be overcome by planning and careful research to ensure that you don't violate some custom in a local territory. A practical way to overcome these problems is to work with your local partners, who will help you overcome the cultural challenges and, at the same time, work to sync in with the global launch of a product or advertising campaign.

Chapter X
The Licensing World

The Licensing World

After a lot of hard work, effort and inspiration, you'll be heartened by the knowledge that this is where your Transmedia project can earn you a lot of money.

Early in 2010, while I was at the TOTY (Toy of the Year Awards), it became clear to me that there is nothing in the media line of business that compares to the potential revenues that exist in the licensing world. Even when you are talking about potential incomes from big budget movies, they are still dwarfed by licensing revenues.

Take, for example, Cars, the blockbuster movie by Pixar. Cars grossed half a billion dollars at the box office back in 2006. It wasn't actually one of Pixar/Disney's most successful movies, but I don't think anyone would argue that this is not an impressive figure. However, this figure gets put in a slightly different perspective when you consider that the revenue raised by licensing Cars merchandise has yielded that amount for every year since 2006 (and it is still growing!).

Comparing the two revenue streams, you can plainly see how box office figures tell just a fraction of a film's financial story. Consider, also, that this is just one example where the revenue from licensing became far bigger than the original project. When you realise that this pattern is replicated across nearly all big feature film releases you begin to get an idea of the overall relationship of the licensing industry to the movie-making industry.

Other evidence of licensing revenues outstripping incomes from the original media product can be seen amongst the biggest media brands. For example, High School Musical and iCarly have been sold to broadcasters all around the globe. Nonetheless, the revenues the production companies get from licensing are still several times higher than the revenues for selling these TV shows worldwide. It can't be emphasised enough, regardless of how successful these types of shows are in terms of DVD sales or feature film box office revenues, the licensing revenues are far, far bigger.

Television toys

Almost inevitably you may think this has led to a situation where the primary focus for some companies has switched from media production to licensing opportunities. This is manifest in a trend where some media companies are making television series purely as loss leaders. This is where the television content is offered free to broadcasters with the proviso that the licensed products are promoted. In essence, the television story is purely a promotional tool to sell toys. This growing trend is particularly pronounced in children's and young people's television, where broadcasters are more often paying very small fees, down to zero, simply because the brand owners want to have their shows (plus repeats) on air so products can be sold.

I've already mentioned the next point, but I want to emphasise how valuable repeated show broadcasts are to the whole licensing venture. This fact has been recognised by the licensing industry experts, who have actually quantified what level of repeat exposure is required to stimulate sales.

This means that, if you want to know what level of exposure your product needs for the Christmas market, they will tell you that you will need X number of television hours, reaching X amount of audience members for each of the weeks in the run-up to the Christmas season. There is an actual mathematical formula for working all this out, down to the last viewer, television hour and market share. I mention this because, when I learned about it for the first time, it struck me that while media producers talk story, these people talk business.

For people working in the licensing world, television is solely a marketing tool, or an advertising platform. While you may know a lot about designing content, these guys make it their business to know exactly how many kids they need to reach to sell a product.

Track record

There is one thing to remember when it comes to considering licensing products. This process takes time. Lots of time, in fact. In our experience, when we were making Sofia's Diary, we were only able to start licensing products (outside of books or a DVD) around the third season. This was because releasing a product based on a brand takes about eighteen months from when you make an agreement to the day the product goes on sale. This time lag means that, if you want to release a product, you will need a long-term plan. Implicit in this is the notion that businesses will only agree to license your brand if they think you're going to be producing the content for broadcast for years to come.

In our situation, it was only after three years that we really started licensing the product. At this point, we were able to start licensing iPod socks, fake tattoos, pyjamas, kids' underwear and a range of other products; this was because we had two key elements in place that persuaded the licenser that they should do business with us.

The first thing that we had was a successful track-record in maintaining and growing a community based on our brand.

The second thing was that we had a commitment from the broadcaster that the show would run in the upcoming years. In effect, we could give comfort to the licenser that the show had a secure future, that the television and radio shows would continue to be on air and that there was a committed online community which would continue to grow. From the licenser's perspective, these facts were crucial to persuading them that agreeing to license our products involved minimum risk on their part.

Plan, don't rush

The fact that the licensing world is a lucrative revenue generator isn't a secret. For that reason, you'll often find people developing a new show and, as soon as it goes to air, immediately expect to have deals to manufacture t-shirts, toys or whatever rolling in. Now, there is nothing wrong about this per se; of course, every single show or production can have its products and, if you can make it work, that's great.

However, in the normal course of events, the challenge is to plan the release of licensed goods within a long-term marketing campaign. There is, of course, this great temptation for people not familiar with the licensing world to rush and get a deal. However, most of these attempts don't work because the licensing companies want long-term marketing strategies showing how you plan to maintain a long-term consumer interest.

This last point is also crucial to grasp because, in effect, what the licensee will be looking for is the chance to make a product that somebody else is marketing. In case you are wondering, you are that somebody doing the marketing. Essentially, this means that the licensee is buying a brand made popular by a successful show and supported by its own marketing strategy. The rules also change according to the age of the target audience:

1 . Kids and Tweenies

If you want to be successful in licensing products aimed at this demographic, the first thing you need is a broadly popular brand. For example, we found with Sofia's Diary that it was no good being popular solely with the target teenage audience. Of course, it is necessary to be popular with the target group and we had, in fact, achieved this when we were only producing web-based content.

However, in addition to being popular with the target audience, we also needed to be a brand that had a certain credibility that was perceived beyond just the teenage demographic. This is important because the purchasers of the licensed goods are not the teenagers but their parents and older relations. Nine times out of ten, you will find adults unfamiliar with a story will be reluctant to endorse a purely web-based phenomenon.

However, once a brand has been broadcast on television, radio or other traditional media, it earns a sort of market credibility. This allows the parent or grandparent purchasers to be more comfortable with the brand which, in turn, makes them more willing to buy its associated products for their sons, granddaughters, etc. Consequently, if you want this purchasing group to buy the products, the brand has to have a measure of credibility and trustworthiness.

We achieved this crucial measure of credibility with Sofia's Diary when we moved from producing web-based to also producing content for the traditional media. Practically speaking, what this meant was that, because Sofia's Diary was broadcast as a television show, it gave confidence to the purchasers of the licensed products to go out and buy them as presents.

Television is a key part of the marketing to this group and this raises another issue around licensing. The fact that television is paramount if you want to license goods is not lost on broadcasters. This realisation explains a growing trend that is seeing more broadcasters looking for a cut of the licensing royalties for products sold in their country. This still typically only happens with commercial broadcasters, but it is a growing phenomenon that you will encounter.

This development, however, might not necessarily be a bad thing for you. Bear in mind that, if the broadcaster is getting a cut on toy sales, the likelihood is that they will broadcast the show on better slots and may even carry some free advertising for the products. This arrangement will see smaller unit revenues for you, but it will also see bigger sales and possibly a reduced advertising budget.

2. Young adults and adults

The rules are slightly different for licensing products for the adult and young adult markets. For starters, children's products are usually sold in supermarkets and big toy chains that usually require a big marketing strategy to support them. For the adult and young adult markets, their toys and products are typically bought in speciality stores such as games or comic book stores.

These products are normally released in smaller quantities. However, perhaps one of the most significant differences is that, whilst licensing to the junior market is green-lighted when it is apparent there is a large number of fans of the product, with the adult market normally the deciding factor in licensing products is whether or not the brand has a dedicated cult following, where many of the followers are willing to buy the product. Though the adult following isn't typically as numerically large as the junior audiences, it can be just as profitable because you can usually charge more per unit. Also, unlike the junior market, your show does not necessarily have to be broadcast on television.

Napoleon Dynamite is a good example of this type of one-off brand that didn't appear on television. Despite its limited availability, as an independent feature film, it still successfully launched a full line of products based on its brand. It could do this because it had created a legion of fans who rented the movie, talked about it afterwards and bought the products (remember the 'Vote for Pedro' t-shirts?).

Napoleon Dynamite is only one example, but it is instructive when understanding how a Transmedia property with only a website or small cable television show can tap a lucrative licensing stream. The key for this type of product, therefore, is not to necessarily have a lot of fans but a number of dedicated followers who will be sufficiently motivated to buy your products. In these cases, usually the revenues are smaller simply because you are selling in smaller quantities. In terms of the distribution channels for this content, usually you will be selling through comic book stores like Forbidden Planet, HMV, FNAC, Amazon or similar internet-based stores.

Agents

I would recommend that, when you are planning to license your brand, instead of contacting the manufacturing company, you should instead get yourself a licensing agent. The licensing agent is a middleman who will carry your brand into the licensing world and use their extensive relationships with the manufacturing world to agree sales deals on your behalf. Normally, the way it works is that, in return for a double digit percentage of the royalties, they are responsible for hammering out the details of your licensing deals. When you are talking about hiring a licensing agent, what you are really looking for is a middleman who knows this world and has built up relationships with manufacturers.

The agents will typically have the rights to demand audits from manufacturers to ensure that they are getting the correct royalty payments. Essentially though, this is where an experienced agent is pretty invaluable as they will know who to trust and when the figures are amiss. The advantage of taking on an agent, who will also have other clients, is that the manufacturer will be less likely to cheat you because they want to maintain their overall relationship with the agent. If, for instance, your agent has agreed a deal for Star Wars products with the manufacturer, it is unlikely that they would risk ruining the relationship over your product.

Overall, the great benefit of an agent is that they know the patterns of the market and, because we live in a global world, your agent will have access to a lot of information and figures. They will know, for instance, that X toy sold so many units in its first week. A good agent will know the ballpark revenue figures for a given period and should be able to spot any discrepancy. This middle man will know what royalties you should be receiving, and will act in your defence because it's in their interest to do so.

Another point to note is that the licensing agents can also act as your marketing partner and can be invaluable when you are trying to manage marketing campaigns across various regions and territories. As we saw in the preceding chapter, this can involve complex challenges and you may want to leave the detail of resolving the marketing launch and its co-ordination with your partners to an expert.

Conclusions

If your Transmedia show doesn't have a huge following and you are thinking about licensing, I would generally advise you to put this thought on hold for a while. I say this because there is no point thinking about licensing in the first year when your first focus should be on developing content and expanding your community.

In addition, in terms of scale you should aim to have your show in several territories before you talk to an agent about licensing.

When you are well-established as an entertainment brand, and you eventually begin to consider licensing, you have to make a decision about how your market will define your options. The first question revolves around trying to define who your market is. For example, ask yourself whether it is aimed at a mass market or at a niche audience.

Once, you are clear on that question, you can address the issue of timing. Regarding this issue, I would advise that you opt into the licensing world after the first year. Again, though, I would emphasise that, whatever the type and profile of your audience, it is always better to have an international presence established if you want to maximise your revenues.

Again, I would say to you that you should really talk to a licensing agent. They will give you the advice and the contacts with key industry people who can solve some of the major licensing issues for you. For instance, they will tell you if your brand has mass market potential or is more suited towards fan-based products.

Lastly on this point, avoid the temptation to do everything on your own. Don't make the t-shirt unless it's just for marketing purposes. What I mean is that I would advise trying to get involved in manufacturing them commercially. Remember, you are not in the textile or toy business and you should leave this to others to do. The licensing world is lucrative but complicated. You can maximise your return on it if you follow some of the advice here and, more importantly, get professional assistance when the time comes.

Chapter XI
The Future

- Lean back vs Lean forward
- Demanding audiences
- Content is hot, channels are not
- The challenges for the Transmedia producer
- Finding your content
- You, the advertisers and change
- Broadcasters and you
- Business models

The Future

In this last chapter, I want to have a look at the likely developments in Transmedia that I think can help inform your plans in the short to medium term.

Lean back vs Lean forward

Since the late 1990s, as the global IT society developed, it could have been described in one sense as being platform-centric; or, to put it another way, it was focused on the devices that we used to consume entertainment. One of the effects of this platform-centric view was that it created very clear delineations between the different genres of content people could expect on different platforms.

What I mean by this is that people were only able to access a specific type of show, information or material by using a specific device. For example, in practical terms this meant that the user expected to receive text messages on mobile phones, or to consume short videos on computers, or watch television shows solely on their television sets, or play games on consoles.

This delineation, as you can readily see these days, has begun to break down as different types of content are now available across a multitude of platforms. As this happens, more and more services, such as BBC iPlayer, Netflix or Hulu, can be consumed on many, many types of devices. This change presents us with an interesting conundrum. If all content is available on a multitude of platforms, the question then arises, how do we know what the user expects when, for example, they turn on their iPad?

For me, this change away from the platform-centric view means that, if you now want to differentiate between types of content, you shouldn't look at the device; instead, you should think about how the user is consuming it.

Accordingly, I think you can broadly classify user experiences into two distinct categories:

(i) The lean back experience.

(ii) The lean forward experience.

The experience a person chooses largely depends on the time and space that a person finds themselves in. For example, If you have an hour to spare at home you are perhaps likely to watch a television programme. Here, the time available (one hour) and the space you find yourself in (your home) determine what experience you will have. Alternatively, whether you have five minutes on a commuter train or ten minutes in your office, here also the time and space available will determine your experience and the type of content you choose to consume.

This categorising of content rests not on what you consume it on but rather the way you consume it. In the past, the lean back versus lean forward categorisation would refer to the platforms that were being used, but now it applies to the user's own experience.

To illustrate this concept a little further, consider how previously you 'leaned in' to use and interact with your computer to, say, work or send emails. This platform would have been always categorised as belonging to the lean forward group. Now, it's pretty commonplace to watch a movie on a computer. The issue, as I've mentioned, is determined not by platform but by the time available and the space that you consume it in. So, if you find yourself at, say, your office or at your home office, doing emails, updating your Facebook profile, navigating the internet, your body leans forward to the screen; you multitask, and each task only catches your attention for a few minutes. Interaction is key for you. Alternatively, you may be on the train heading home, and you connect your notebook to a 3G internet dongle, connect to an internet video player, make the video window full screen, and your body leans back in your seat. You just do one thing: watch video.

In the 'lean back' experience, the user doesn't interact with the platform, doesn't switch between activities every few minutes, doesn't check emails and doesn't interact or participate in the story. Instead, the user presses 'play' on the movie or one-hour episode, leans back and watches in the exact same way they would on a television. However, now you can do this using your notebook, your tablet or even on your iPhone. Therefore, you can see the computer can belong to either the lean forward, or lean back experience - what defines it is the actions of the user, not the design of the device.

In fact, when you think about it, this lean back experience can be on any single device, be it a mobile phone, iPad, computer, whatever. This illustrates the enduring attraction of the lean back experience, as people watch content for a longer period of time where they don't want to be distracted by other activities. All they want to do is choose the device they are going to use (be it phone, television or computer) and then 'sit back and enjoy'. The practice is the same as the traditional television viewing experience; the only difference is that the content may now be consumed from the comfort of the couch at home, in the office, on the bus or on a plane. Simply put, the lean back experience is the viewer in relaxed pose, consuming content in a wider variety of locations on a wider variety of devices.

Let us consider the lean forward experience. In this case, the user is typically way more active, clicking on a variety of options, finding out more, interacting more and so on. This experience can be enjoyed on all those lean back devices that we mentioned. For instance, whether you are using your computer or your iPad, you can interact with internet content or, alternatively, watch a television series. Nowadays, because you also have products like Google TV, you can enjoy a lean forward experience with a television set, further illustrating the breakdown in the notion of specific contents for specific devices. In fact, with the advent of internet-connected television sets, you can now update your Facebook profile or enter messenger conversations all at the same time, while your favourite TV show plays in the background.

This trend isn't as yet complete, but I think it's fair to say that you will find content increasingly falling into either of these two categories. Consequently, when you're developing a Transmedia product, think about these patterns as you opt to include some lean back content or, alternatively, lean forward content that may be consumed on the myriad of available devices. I would say to you, therefore, that as a producer you need to think about balancing these experiences and not to focus on the devices that will be used.

Practically speaking, this means you need to think about these user experiences. Short form, interactivity and engagement is carried out more in a lean forward type of experience, while a lean back experience, such as a movie or a one-hour TV episode, needs to be more 'entertaining'. By combining both experiences, you can build a loyal audience where they can engage with characters and your storyworld both in short periods of time during their day, and in more entertainment-oriented long form episodes that can be only made available once a week.

This also means that, as you will be producing different contents, you will sometimes be asking your audience to move from a lean forward to a lean back experience. Requesting them to make this jump has its own potential for losing audience as they make the transition. However, in the future this loss won't be as great as they won't necessarily have to change devices in the process.

Demanding audiences

The second big challenge for the Transmedia producer is the ongoing change we are seeing as audiences move from consuming entertainment in a traditional linear to an 'on demand' fashion.

Consider, in the past, how a typical media consumer would get up in the morning and listen to the radio and go to work. They may read a newspaper during their coffee break or on their way home. When they arrive home, they would watch television and consume the television programmes that the broadcaster selected for that evening.

This pattern is fast becoming a thing of the past. With radio, for instance, the podcast is becoming more popular so you don't have to tune in at a specific time to listen to your favourite DJ or radio programme. The newspaper industry is also adapting, as more and more of their content is consumed not on paper but on demand from their websites or on iPad, eBook reader's or other tablet computer devices. Also, many people have apps on their phones that allow them to consume news and information at the time they choose to consume it, even as it occurs if they so wish.

This will, I think, affect the traditional way we view television in a very radical way. Consider the fact that we are currently witnessing a growing trend where, for a significant minority, television content is consumed on demand rather than on schedule. For example, witness the growing demand for BBC iPlayer services (as a percentage of what is broadcast live on the BBC).

Also, a large and growing percentage of the television audience have personal video recorders that allow them to opt out of linear broadcasts and view the content at their own convenience. In addition to these facilities, there are 'catch-up television' services, which are internet players that you can use to access programme if you miss it live. These catch-up services usually provide the material free for approximately one week after the original broadcast, after which time the user can access the content on a pay-to-view basis.

We are also, as it happens, in the midst of another shift that began in the 1980s and 1990s when people first started to use pay-to-view options on television. In this period, there has been a huge increase in the number of television channels from just a few to hundreds of available channels.

Perhaps, though, the most radical change in how we use television isn't the increased number of channels, but more the way we will choose what we are going to view. In other words, there is an increased trend not to opt for a menu of channels that air certain contents at certain times. Instead, viewers are being offered services that allow them to choose the content that they wish to view. This bespoke television schedule may then be accessed by the viewer on an on demand basis. Essentially, the service allows the viewer to design their own television schedule. What it means, in practical terms, is that you don't have to have a package of channels; rather, you have an on-demand box that allows you to pick the shows you want to view.

This phenomenon will also likely involve us changing how we pay for our television content. As things stand, the user can either pay per show or pay a subscription for a certain amount of content. Up until now, the television payment model involved paying approximately twenty-five euros for a base channel pack and then an additional amount for each additional channel or package of channels. What this usually resulted in was a situation where customers were increasingly unhappy paying a monthly television subscription fee of, say, eighty euros for a large number of channels that they rarely watch.

As consumers have reacted against having access to a large number of unwatched television channels, they have, where the service is available, reacted positively to the idea of paying for their own bespoke television schedule. Viewers have indicated that they increasingly want a box or device that allows them to view their own choice of content; this makes more sense, and may be cheaper, than having a huge range of services that they barely interact with.

Content is hot, channels are not

This development is a big challenge for speciality channels as the content becomes more important than the channel brand identity. This trend has, of course, been underway for some time as people increasingly abandon linear television. For example, up to a few years ago television ratings only measured live broadcast viewers. However, because of the change in viewer habits, they have to also measure viewers who access content on delayed transmission, on demand, on personal video recorders or on the internet. These figures aren't insignificant either; in the United States, depending on the show, the numbers watching on the new on demand services can be up to 40 per cent of the total audience. Increasingly, broadcasters have found that more cult shows, such as True Blood, will especially display this pattern of audience behaviour.

Whatever the type of show, a fairly universal trend is emerging where the brand of the show is becoming far more important than the channel brand. Studies show this trend to be a growing phenomenon, in that it is not just for kids viewing content on the internet, but is in reality an across the board development, as all demographic groups shift their viewing behaviour to varying extents.

As the demand for this type of viewing choice grows more and more, services are being supplied to satisfy it. Connected TV Services are being provided as most television sets now mostly have internet connections. Services such as these, which allow viewers to download content, have two significant consequences. Firstly, the price barrier that accompanied the old subscription model disappears and, secondly, the simplicity of accessing your own desired content becomes the norm.

As the linear, traditional viewing model shrinks, you may wonder if there is any future at all for mainstream television. I think that, while it is a declining way of accessing content, it will in the medium term focus on the big, catch-all television events such as X Factor and the Eurovision Song Contest. Essentially this means it will focus on those big events that people like to experience live, where you don't want to take the chance of missing who gets voted off. The same is true of big sporting events that people usually want to view live and which consequently unite huge audiences viewing it simultaneously.

The trend, therefore, will be for the big event to be a live television event because it is something that doesn't make sense to supply on demand. The content of these events often only make sense when everyone is watching live and the audience is united around a specific timeframe. Imagine, for instance, if American Idol was an on-demand show; the consequence of this would be that the voting would have to take place over a longer period, say seven days. In all likelihood, having this sort of prolonged results process isn't something that the audience would respond positively to, so it just wouldn't make sense to have this sort of show on demand.

There are, of course, many types of content that are well suited to the on-demand, non-linear method. For instance, almost all documentaries, dramas, comedies, even the news can be accessed when the user wants it rather than when the broadcaster supplies it.

The Challenges for the Transmedia producer

With all this change, the good news for the Transmedia producer is that, in the near future, the brand of your show will be more important than the channel that broadcasts it. It also, of course, increases the opportunities for your brand to reach a global audience.

However, the big challenge for you is how you can ensure that audiences will find your content and notice your brand. If you are to tackle this issue successfully, marketing will be absolutely key. The fact that your show is available on a lot of devices doesn't mean everyone will watch it. This fact of life means that you will still have to employ all the methods and devices that we have previously mentioned to ensure that audiences know exactly what your brand is and how they can access your content. As a practical step, I would say that it's important to keep a focus on using social media as well as other entities with prebuilt audiences, so you can build the buzz surrounding your content and generally let people know about your brand.

The other challenge that arises for the Transmedia producer comes about from the huge expansion in the availability of broadband services. Until now, the quality of the viewing experience was limited as video demanded a lot of bandwidth. Now, however, optical fibre means this bandwidth limitation is not an issue, thus allowing 3D or HD content to be far more widely available. As these technical limitations are vanishing and broadband increasingly becomes the norm, changes are also taking place in the quality of mobile devices. Mobile devices, which were once clunky, are now slick, high-quality devices with better interactive experiences allowing you to consume video satisfactorily in any location. The upshot of all this is that, as these technical limitations vanish and devices like the iPad with broadband connection become more common, people won't need different devices to access specific contents. Instead, you will see a growing trend for people to consume a variety of different contents and experiences from one single device.

Another important change for the Transmedia producer revolves around how people select and consume internet content. For the first ten years of mainstream internet use, it was organised around particular portals which were, in effect, the 'gatekeepers' of the internet. This meant sites like Yahoo, MSN or particular newspapers were like central points that provided lots of information and acted as starting points for people searching for the content that interested them.

The social media phenomenon has, however, revolutionised this pattern of internet behaviour. Now, instead of going to a central point like MSN and accessing the suggested content they find there, people are consuming material because it was recommended by their friends. People are accessing content because their own activity on a social media or a friend's recommendation allows them to find new shows, magazines or comedy pieces. As a consequence of this, the content you access is less dependent on what a media portal recommends but, rather, is more influenced by what your friends are doing. Again, as we mentioned before, this highlights how important social media are to creating the buzz around your show and drawing viewers to your content.

Finding your content

Back in its early days, the internet acted like a directory for the content it contained. It could do this because the internet was small enough to be indexed. However, as the internet has since become so vast, this sort of directory-based search isn't possible now. Instead of browsing through directories, now it is the search keywords that have become vital for locating desired content.

Accordingly, it is search words like, for instance, the name of an actor in your show, that becomes more important for people searching for content. We mentioned before that there is a big benefit to using a well-known actress or actor (even for a short time) on your show because their name is likely to be searched. Whenever they are searched, your content will appear on the search results.

Another way of attracting people to your content is to be recommended either in social media, as we mentioned earlier, or in playlists or top ten lists that are compiled by other users. Friends' recommendations and endorsements by fans are, in fact, becoming more powerful than the traditional search.

Another point to note is the facility seen on iTunes, Amazon and Youtube where you get offered suggested content on a 'if you watched this you will like that' basis. Using key talent in your show will increase the chances of your content being accessed in this fashion.

We spoke before about how important it is for Transmedia producers to know how to market their content, and also how the game-plan for getting your brand noticed has changed beyond recognition. In this new world, you are not fighting for a primetime television slot, instead you are fighting to get noticed amongst a great sea of varied content.

You should bear in mind the fact that we live in a world with a vast oversupply of content. As it grew, this oversupply of content created a problem for anyone looking for material on the internet. The search, therefore, should be seen as the solution to this problem, allowing people to find what they are looking for. There are a variety of ways that you can maximise your rate of return in internet searches, which is in itself a fairly specialised area of expertise.

You, the advertisers and change

Something that may help Transmedia producers is the fact that the advertising industry is being forced to change its entire approach to television. Until recently, TV advertising has acted along the same lines as when it was established decades ago. During this time, advertising occurred between shows and the advertisers could be fairly confident of reaching their target consumers.

However, as we are moving to an on-demand world, the notion of ad-breaks simply doesn't exist anymore. Accordingly, after successfully applying the same formula for fifty years, the advertising industry is reluctantly shifting towards the notion of placing advertisements embedded within the shows. This change will see traditional television advertising fall from the hugely commanding position it now occupies. It often surprises people when they realise that typically 90 per cent of most advertising budgets is on television advertising. However, for audiences aged 15-45, more time is spent accessing content on the internet than watching television.

As this shift develops, you will see advertisers not approaching the broadcasters but, instead, directing their attentions to the content producers. The change will also see a general move towards advertisers engaging with all the content types that people are accessing. This means there will be an increasing trend of advertisers contacting Transmedia producers about placing adverts within their various genres of content, whether that be the webisode, social network site or television series.

Broadcasters and you

As the change from linear television takes hold, broadcasters too are facing a world where they will have to exist in a completely different way. The smarter broadcaster will survive by seizing the notion of a broadcaster that represents a particular editorial concept. In this way, the broadcaster will provide its imprimatur to a certain type and style of content. This is because a particular broadcaster can provide a level of familiarity and assurance to the viewer, so that the viewer knows when they go to a particular broadcaster they know what they are going to get. What is likely to happen, as this trend develops, is that broadcasters, which in a way no longer make sense in a non-linear world, can instead provide the viewer with an identifiable editorial imprint or brand. The broadcaster's editorial approach will, of course, guide their selection of content in order to ensure it is consistent with the viewer's expectations.

In practical terms, this means that someone who is interested in documentaries may want to go to the Discovery channel, where they can access a selection of the content that they know will interest them. To take an overview of the broadcaster's structure in this new television world, it wouldn't make sense to have more than one linear channel. This linear channel will operate alongside the broadcaster's specialised content, which will be available on demand. The linear channel will be used to promote a bigger catalogue of related content that audiences can then watch on demand.

Despite all the changes, I think these broadcasters will survive. They will continue to commission the shows and pay for the content that best fits their editorial line. In addition, I should point out that advertisers may have an existing relationship with the traditional broadcaster and are consequently familiar with the broadcaster's standards and policies. This is important, because this relationship may make them more likely to deal with those producers who are supplying content to the established broadcasters. Familiarity and trust play a significant part in these decisions and I think the advertisers will, at least in the early stages, want to deal with producers who are working with familiar broadcasters. This will tend (at least in the short term) to maintain the broadcaster's power advantage in the non-linear television world.

As this change eventually plays out, your favourite broadcaster will become like a playlist providing, on demand, the different shows you like to watch. People are, of course, naturally attracted to this sort of recommended playlist that comes from a familiar source. These recommendations may be compared to safe zones, where they can have confidence that they will like the content because it is recommended by the broadcaster. Because they have the brands that audiences identity with, in all likelihood they will not disappear. This means, for instance, that if you want a documentary and you like the documentaries that are provided by the BBC, you can go to BBC Documentary and choose from one of the programmes on offer there.

Business models

How we pay for our content is something that also needs to change if we are to fully realise the potential of the available media technology. As things stand, the business model for accessing television content and internet content has been left somewhat antiquated by the technological changes.

What this means is that, in the recent past, the only way to get different types of content was to use different devices. Accordingly, the business model for accessing content is based on the user paying according to what device they are using. However, as we have seen, you can now access various types of content on a single device. As this change takes place it doesn't make sense to pay one fee for internet access on your computer, another fee to have internet content on your television and still another fee to access internet content on your phone.

As the delineations between what constitutes a television, computer and mobile device become ever more blurry, in reality you should pay for a single unified fee for content access. There are straws in the wind that show this is changing; for instance, once you purchase content from iTunes you can move it from one device to another free of charge. However, most others don't yet allow for this type of free movement. As things change we will have to wean ourselves away from this focus on device.

What I think will happen eventually is that you will be able to buy a subscription for a bundle of content, be it music, television shows, movies, games or whatever. Once you have purchased content, you will then be able to access it on all your devices. In a world where you can do this, pay based on what particular device you use just won't make sense. Eventually, because it will be far more user-friendly, I think we will see the one fee for your content model take hold.

What is also disappearing is the notion that you can successful limit content by traditional geographical barriers. Also, people are increasingly less likely to buy into the notion that they must wait to access content that is already available in another part of the globe. Another significant change can be seen in the shrinking windows for releasing content. In the United States, for example, independent movies will premiere during a weekend in theatres and be available a few days later on video on demand services.

I mention all these changes because they are part of a great revolution in the way we all consume media content. In a sense, they are changes that can easily overwhelm producers who are used to operating in the traditional, stable media environment. However, as not responding to change isn't an option, I truly believe that Transmedia skills empower the media producer with the skills necessary to connect with the audience.

These skills also empower you as a creator because, in the Transmedia business model, you can own your creation, develop it as a brand and monetise it for your gain. Because you create your brand, you invest in it and develop it, you are therefore in control. You may find that, in the short term, it means more work for less money; but in the long term, you are in control and have the opportunity to realise the revenues and returns available to you from the Transmedia world... You are creating and nurturing.

Appendixes

Appendix I: Further Reading

The Pixel Report

www.thepixelreport.org

The Pixel Report is brought to you by Power to the Pixel's Liz Rosenthal & Tishna Molla. The website is devoted to showcasing new forms of storytelling, film-making and cross-media business development that is in tune with an audience-centred digital era. It is an essential tool for content creators, a vital resource for policy-makers & funding bodies and a unique guide for anyone interested in the future of film and the media.

The Workbook Project

www.workbookproject.com

The WorkBook Project (WBP) is for those who want to be creative in the digital age. The WBP, through its website, R&D projects such as festival From Here to Awesome and roving conference DIY Days, provides insight into the process of funding, creating, distributing and sustaining as a creator of media (film, games, music, design, software).

JawboneTV

www.jawbone.tv

JawboneTV is a collective resource and project showcase that tightly embraces those things on the progressive edge of digital and interactive narrative—the good, the bad, and the bad-ass of story in the digital age. Operations are based out of Toronto, Can ada, with contributors from New York, London, Sydney, Vancouver, and Los Angeles to name but a few.

ARG Net

www.argn.com

The Alternate Reality Gaming Network is the largest and most complete news resource available for players of online collaborative Alternate Reality Games. For many years, this site was the central hub for an affiliate network of sites that were independently owned and operated by volunteers for the enjoyment of themselves and the ARG community.

Appendix II: Further Training

Power to the Pixel

www.powertothepixel.com

Power to the Pixel is a company helping international filmmakers and the film industry make the transition to a cross-media digital age. Its services include consultancy, training and events as well as information and analysis of the changing international market. It is run and supported by some of the most experienced cross-media pioneers, professionals and filmmakers in the world.

Transmedia Next

www.transmedianext.com

Transmedia Next is an advanced training programme aimed at experienced media professionals in the art, craft and business of storytelling in the 21st century.

Transmedia Lab @ Storylabs

storylabs.us/transmedia-lab

StoryLabs were formed in Australia, Canada the US and UK aim is to pioneer digital content creation, strategy and innovation through strong, multi media story engagement.

Multiplatform Business School

mpbs.mediaschool.es

One of the foremost training and R&D centres in Europe, the Media Business School has the backing of the MEDIA PLUS Programme of the European Union, the Instituto de la Cinematografía y de las Artes Audiovisuales de España (ICAA), the government of Andalucía and the City of Ronda (Malaga). The Media Business School also has the support of various leading companies and key players in the European audiovisual industry.

The Transmedia Learning Network

www.transmedialearningnetwork.org

The Transmedia Learning Network is an independent, not-for-profit organisation whose members include an international group of film- and media-schools and faculties, forward-looking companies and organisations. Together we develop and deliver transmedia curricula, education and training, and initiate and support innovative transmedia projects.

443008

CPSIA information can be obtained at www.ICGtesting.com
Printed in the USA
LVOW11s1537111113

360873LV00004B/820/P

9 780956 750006